Living Lawns

design • restore • enjoy

David and Charles

Andrew McIndoe

A David & Charles Book

Published in association with Westland Garden Health

Copyright © David & Charles 2006

David & Charles is an F+W Publications Inc. Company
4700 East Galbraith Road Cincinnati, OH 45236
First published in the UK in 2006

Text Copyright © Andrew McIndoe 2006

Andrew McIndoe has asserted his right to be identified as author of this work in accordance
with the Copyright, Designs and Patents Act, 1988.

A catalogue record for this book is available from the British Library
ISBN-13: 978-0-7153-2703-6
ISBN-10: 0-7153-2703-8

Printed in Great Britain by William Gibbons Ltd
for David & Charles
Brunel House Newton Abbot Devon

Produced for David & Charles by
OutHouse Publishing
Winchester Hampshire SO22 5DS

For OutHouse Publishing:
Project Editor Sue Gordon   Art Editor Robin Whitecross

For David & Charles:
Commissioning Editor Mic Cady   Editorial Assistant Emily Rae   Designer Sarah Clark
Production Director Roger Lane

Visit our website at www.davidandcharles.co.uk

David & Charles books are available from all good bookshops; alternatively you can contact
our Orderline on 0870 9908222 or write to us at FREEPOST EX2 110, D&C Direct,
Newton Abbot TQ12 4ZZ (no stamp required UK mainland);
US customers call 800-289-0963 and Canadian customers call 800-840-5220.

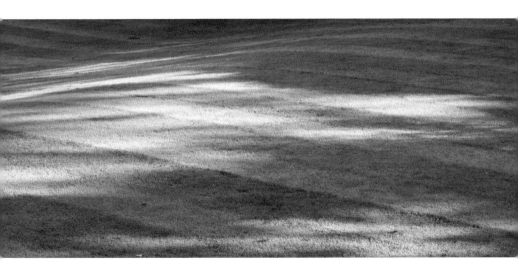

Contents

Introduction

A lawn is a plantation: thousands of individual grass plants all competing for air, light, water and nutrients. In other areas of the garden we consider individual plants. We give them space, preventing the stronger from overpowering the weaker subjects. We prepare the soil, cultivate, feed, water, thin and space seedlings.

The lawn we treat differently. We use it as a surface to walk upon and to play upon, and we expect it to look green, fresh and verdant regardless of how hard we prune it and how erratically we water and feed it. Start treating the grass plants in the lawn as we would other plants and we should see better results.

Lawncare is not difficult, and it need not be arduous. It is a matter of identifying any problems, implementing a remedy and then introducing a care regime to prevent those problems re-occurring. Once you get to grips with managing your lawn, it all becomes part of the enjoyment of gardening rather than an additional task that interferes with it. This book will show you how.

In today's garden, grass can be more than a flat green area. A lawn is not just stripes and straight edges. It is usually a vital part of the structure of the garden as a whole, essential space to balance the vertical mass of the surrounding planting. It is space that can easily be made more appealing, and more interesting, not only by caring for it properly but also by adjusting its shape and improving its association with the beds and borders. And, to make your lawn even livelier, and less formal, you can add other plants to the grass mixture: bulbs and meadow flowers transform the space into a part of the planting that welcomes wildlife and provides a link with the countryside.

Living Lawns will help you to get more from what is perhaps the easiest-to-cultivate and most dominant plant in your garden and in our lives – GRASS!

Andrew McIndoe

Left: Broad grass steps add interest to a sloping lawn. Above from the top: Grass can create a soft, living pathway. Wildflowers in grass. *Crocus tommasinianus.*

Designing a lawn

A lawn is usually the dominant feature in a garden so its shape and design need consideration, whether you are starting from scratch or reviewing an established garden. Planning needs to take into account the maintenance of the lawn, particularly when it comes to the mowing.

Proportions As a rule, the most pleasing gardens consist of two-thirds 'space' and one-third planting. This space can be made up of gravel, paving, water, ground-cover plants and, of course, grass. However, in many gardens the proportion of space is greater than this: too much paving and lawn, insufficient planting. This draws attention to the lawn, putting undue emphasis on its shape and design. Reducing the amount of grass and adding depth to the planting integrates the lawn into the overall garden design.

Shape The shape of the lawn is obvious at all times of year but especially so in winter, when it becomes the dominant patch of green in the garden.

Once a lawn and borders are installed, most gardeners make few changes to the layout. However, adjusting the shape of the lawn need not be a major task – and it might transform an ordinary garden into a very much more pleasing one.

The shape of a lawn is especially visible in winter.

Often the shape of the lawn is determined by the shape of the plot: rectangular garden, rectangular lawn. This results in borders of even width and long, straight lines that do nothing for the interest and perspective of the garden. Simply taking the corners off a rectangular lawn and making the lawn more elliptical makes the beds in the corners of the garden deeper, allowing more substantial planting and creating a more interesting picture. Seen from the house, an elliptical lawn seems to open up in the centre and taper in the distance. This increases the perspective, making the plot seem longer.

A similar effect can be created by using a round lawn in a square garden. This is a simple formula that works and is pleasing to the eye.

Avoid complicated edges In an attempt to make a lawn more interesting, many gardeners give the borders wavy edges. These look contrived and fussy, and become even more complicated when the plants in the borders start to grow. Curves should be soft and sweeping, and lead the eye; they need to be there for a reason. Lawns with too many curves and difficult corners are hard to mow and, unless an undue amount of time is invested in maintenance, will look more and more untidy as the season progresses.

Formal lawns Formal lawns, especially square and rectangular ones, need to be in perfect condition to look good; remember this when planning your garden. Regular and accurate mowing, careful lawn husbandry, time and effort are all needed to maintain the effect. If you do not have the time or dedication for this type of lawn, opt for a more informal design. The lawn can still be beautiful, but it does not need to be quite so immaculate!

Above: Use pen and paper to design your lawn. Below: An immaculate formal design.

7

Practicality When designing the shape of your lawn it is important to think about certain practical issues.

● Entrances into the garden from paths, patios and gateways that lead directly onto the lawn may cause undue wear and tear and become impractical in wet weather. Consider transitional areas of paving or coarse gravel.

● Beds and borders need to be large enough to accommodate the planting. Plants spilling onto the grass may look attractive but if you have to hold them back every time you mow they soon become a nuisance.

● You need to be able to manoeuvre and turn the mower easily: awkward corners are difficult to maintain. If you have to walk over a flowerbed to turn the mower, think again: change the shape of the lawn or the bed.

● Avoid positioning ornaments, pots and heavy furniture as features directly on the lawn. If they are in the right place, incorporate a hard surface to accommodate them; if they are not, put them somewhere else. A birdbath that has to be moved off the grass every time the mower is used is an obstacle. In time you will leave it in position and mow around it. There will soon be long, untidy grass around the ornament and you will need shears or a strimmer to cut it: very labour intensive.

Above: Beds should be shaped to allow easy mowing. Below: A pot is incorporated into the lawn on an area of brick and stone.

● Grass paths between flowerbeds, or between beds and paved areas, walls or fences, must be wide enough to allow easy mowing. The same applies to the spaces between any trees and shrubs planted in grass.

If you are designing a new garden, it is worth planning any narrow grass areas to, say, two or three mower widths: a path just wider than twice the width of the mower needs half as much mowing again as a path that is slightly less than twice the width of the mower. Similarly, narrow paths, not wide enough to accommodate the mower, become a real maintenance problem.

Mowing edges Mowing edges make cutting the grass easier. These are transitional areas between the lawn and other parts of the garden. A 10cm (4in) gap alongside a path or patio, filled with gravel to a lower level than the surface of both the lawn and the paving, makes it easy to mow up to the edge of the grass, as does a brick or gravel edge around planted areas. The latter also prevents damage to the plants in the beds. If the level of the mowing strip is slightly below the surface of the grass, you may not need to use edging shears.

To achieve a really sharp edge and retain an accurate shape, use a good-quality metal or plastic lawn edging. Any lawn edging should be inserted into the ground so that there is at least the same amount of edging below the ground as there is above it. The top of the edging should be just below the surface of the turf – not above it, as this will look unnatural and obtrusive.

Thin, flimsy plastic edging is easily dislodged by mowing and will detract from the look of the lawn; heavier-gauge edging does a useful job and keeps the lawn edge sharp.

Paths If you are designing from scratch, it is worth considering a path as a mowing strip down at least one side of the lawn. This will form a boundary between the planting and the grass and at the same time allow access to the flowerbed for maintenance. A path that is a dominant feature – as it is when it goes across the middle of a lawn – needs to lead somewhere: a path along the edge of the lawn is softer and less intrusive.

Above: A gravel edge to a bed makes mowing and cutting edges easier. Below: A brick path through the lawn can be used as a cutting edge.

Stepping stones are an alternative to a path for access across a lawn. These can look good as long as the stones are big enough and tie in with other paving and stone used in the garden. They need to be the right distance apart for walking across, and should be set in a logical path rather than dotted around randomly in an attempt to create an informal effect.

Set the stones into the ground so that the surface of the stepping stone is slightly below the surface of the lawn. The mower can then pass easily over the top of the stone without causing damage to lawn or mower.

Starting from scratch

All gardeners initiate an area of grass at some point, whether they are extending an existing lawn by a few inches to change its shape or starting a new lawn from scratch. As with any other type of planting, the future condition and appearance of the lawn is dependent on good ground preparation. Timescale comes into the equation: turf is the favourite option if an instant lawn is required; if speed is not essential, seed may be better as it is likely to produce more predictable results in the longer term.

Cultivation in preparation for a new lawn is the secret of success.

Getting ready for new grass

Thorough ground preparation, including removing weeds, cultivating and improving the soil, addressing drainage issues, and levelling, is essential at the outset.

Weeds Firstly you must rid the site of perennial and annual weeds. This can only be successfully achieved in the growing season, by applying a non-residual, systemic herbicide to actively growing weeds. Leave them until they have died down completely, indicating that the roots have been killed. On heavily infested sites wait until the weeds re-grow and then repeat the process.

Seeds of annual weeds are present in the soil. When soil is disturbed by cultivation, the seeds come to the surface and germinate. New lawns often incorporate masses of annual weeds. These are easily wiped out by mowing, but to prevent further spread this must be done before they set seed.

Cultivation The site must be thoroughly dug over or rotovated. If the soil is at all compacted beneath the surface, a rotovator will not solve the problem as it only cultivates to a fixed depth. It is essential that any compacted soil below the surface is broken up, by digging if necessary, to allow free drainage when the lawn is laid.

All soils can be improved at this stage by incorporating organic matter. This can be well-rotted farmyard manure, garden compost, composted green household waste (see pages 54–56), or any organic soil conditioner. On heavy clay, incorporate sharp grit and organic soil conditioner; on light soils, just the organic matter. Cultivate, leave for a week or so and re-cultivate.

Drainage   Proper drainage is essential for all good lawns. On a poorly drained site where water lies on the surface at times, land drains are the only solution. If in doubt, seek professional advice.

Smaller lawns on heavy soil can often be drained by raising them slightly above the adjoining ground level. A gravel edging to the lawn will carry away excess moisture.

Levelling   Do not hurry the ground preparation process; skimping on time and effort at the beginning will cost hours later.

● Get rid of stones – they will keep coming to the surface and can damage the blades of your mower. Hand-picking them is the only answer.

● Now the ground needs to be firmed, but not compacted. You can achieve this by taking shuffling steps over the area or by laying a plank of wood on the ground and walking over it several times. Gradually move the plank across the site until you have firmed the whole area. If you do not firm the ground, it may settle unevenly later, resulting in dips and bumps.

Absolute levelling of the site is essential, whether you choose seed or turf. Dips and bumps do not disappear when the grass has grown; they are obstacles when mowing. An uneven site will result in scalped areas and patches of long grass. This is difficult to correct later, so get it right at the outset.

Final preparation   The final stage in ground preparation is the same whether you are opting for seed or for turf. You need to produce a fine, level 'tilth' on which to sow the seed or lay the turf. For this you will need a wide garden rake – and some patience.

● Rake the surface backwards and forwards in all directions, breaking up lumps of soil and removing any remaining stones.

● If your soil is poor, it is worth investing in sufficient finely graded loam to provide ideal growing conditions at the soil surface. Turf suppliers usually supply this in bulk bags and will advise on quantity. Small bags of topsoil are available at garden centres. Distribute it evenly over the site and rake level with a wide rake.

● A week or so before you lay the turf or sow seed add a general lawn fertiliser (see pages 40–41) and rake into the surface. If it does not rain, water the ground gently but thoroughly.

Seed or turf?

A new lawn can be created using either seed or turf. Each has its merits and both can produce a beautiful lawn. Seed is cheaper; you have more choice of types and more control. Turf is quicker.

Whichever you choose, buy the right product for the job and never compromise on quality. It is surprising how much we spend on aspects of the garden such as furniture compared to what we spend on the lawn.

Grass seed should be sown thinly and evenly – something like this.

Seed

Decide what you will be using the lawn for and then choose the type of seed mixture accordingly:

● *A lawn to look upon* Choose a mix of fine tufted grasses, such as fescues. The lawn will have a bright green colour and fine texture.

● *A lawn to walk upon* Choose a mixture of fine grasses, such as fescues, mixed with dwarf perennial ryegrasses that grow horizontally and are harder wearing.

● *A lawn to play upon* Choose a mixture of dwarf perennial ryegrasses. The colour may not be as bright and fresh as when fine tufted grasses are used, but the lawn stays looking good despite heavy use and the grass is resistant to wear.

Remember...

Germinating grass seed and newly laid turf require plenty of water. The best times to lay turf and sow seed are March or April and September or October. Avoid hot dry periods; the effort is wasted: dried-out turf results in gaps, dried-out seed can result in uneven or little germination.

Buy good-quality grass seed, not necessarily the cheapest. Make sure that the seed you buy is current season's stock. The germination of grass seed deteriorates rapidly with age and results can be disappointing if seeds are sown when they are old.

Grass breeding has produced seed mixtures that cope with many different growing situations, including remarkably adverse conditions. Choose special mixes for specific areas of the garden, particularly shady or dry. The same principle applies whether you are selecting grass seed for the lawn or plants for the beds and borders: the secret of success is to choose the right plant for the situation.

Sowing adjoining areas with different seed mixes Work out the areas to be seeded with the different mixes and buy a little more seed than you need for each. At the edge of each area, sow the seed thinly, blending it into the mix for the adjoining area. The transition should be unnoticeable.

A fine grass seed mixture will produce a bright emerald green lawn with a velvety texture.

How much seed should I put down? Grass-seed packets always carry specific instructions: follow them. It is tempting to sow more thickly than recommended: this is counter-productive and results in an overcrowded lawn.

Sowing a large area If you are going to sow grass seed on a large area buy, borrow or hire a spreader suitable for seed. Sow lightly once up and down the lawn, then once across at right angles to the first application.

How soon can a newly sown lawn be cut? Cut as soon as little soil is visible and the grass is 4–5cm (1.5–2in) long. Start off with the mower on a high setting.

Choose special seed mixes for specific areas of the garden, particularly shady or dry

Turf

Turf offers the nearest solution to an instant lawn: lay it, water it and there it is, almost ready to use.

Turf is heavy and arduous to lay over large areas. If you have no experience, employ a contractor; any turf supplier worth his salt will recommend one.

Preparing the ground Always prepare the ground before you order your turf (see pages 10–11).

Buying the turf Buy from a specialist turf grower, not from a supplier who cuts a field and digs it up.

Turf needs to be laid as soon as possible after delivery; it deteriorates quickly, particularly in warm weather.

> **Tip...** Most specialist suppliers have websites that give excellent information on selecting the right turf, ordering the right quantity and laying the turf correctly.

Cheap turf is rarely grown for lawn use. Do not be afraid to ask your supplier where the turf came from and what grasses it contains. Each turf covers anything from 1 to 3sq m (1.2 to 3.5sq yd), according to what you buy. You will need to hire equipment to help lay the larger turves; this will be available from your supplier. Although larger turves require fewer joints, smaller ones are easier to manage. Always buy a little more than you need, to allow for trimming; your supplier will advise on this.

● Turf deteriorates quickly when stacked, especially in hot weather: have it delivered when you can lay it immediately. If you find you cannot lay it for a few days, open out the rolls and lay them flat to allow air and light to reach the grass.

Laying the turf You will need a sharp spade or edging iron to trim the edges, but a stout pair of scissors or an old kitchen knife is usually best for cutting the turves at any internal joints.

● Ideally start from the furthest edge. If there is a straight edge to the lawn, lay a row of turves along that first. Lay subsequent rows, staggering the joints and butting the turves tightly against one another without bending or stretching the turves. If the edge is gently curved, fit turves around the edge of the lawn first and then fill in the centre, running in straight lines up and down the lawn, staggering the joints.

● As the turves are laid, flatten them by laying a heavy plank on them and either walking on it carefully or tapping it gently with a rubber mallet.

● Water thoroughly over the next few weeks until roots are established.

How soon can newly laid turf be cut? Most people wait too long before cutting a newly laid lawn. If the new grass is growing well it can be cut after a week. Remember the rule: never reduce the height by more than one-third.

A lawn in a planter

The fresh green quality of grass adds life to any outdoor space. In small gardens, which may be paved areas without any soil for planting directly into the ground, grass – like any other plant – can be grown in a planter.

A shallow bowl or box is ideal. Fill it with general-purpose potting compost, ideally containing loam. Lightly firm the surface, which should be only very slightly below the top of the container. In round containers you can gently mound the soil to make it slightly higher in the centre.

Sow grass seed evenly across the surface and water the seed and compost regularly with a fine watering-can rose or hose-end sprinkler. The grass will need regular clipping with either lawn shears or one-handed topiary shears.

Fritillarias are lovely spring flowers to add to a lawn in a planter.

Tip... A container lawn can be underplanted with species crocus, fritillaries or dwarf narcissi for extra spring colour.

This is a great way to introduce green space into any area of the garden where it is lacking. A container filled with grass makes a wonderful companion planter for trimmed and trained subjects in pots, such as box balls. Although often used in contemporary planting schemes, grass planters also sit happily in traditional settings.

Lawncare by season

Just like the other plants in the garden, grass has different needs according to the time of year. Each season brings with it certain tasks vital to keep the lawn in peak condition and looking good.

Spring

As the grass starts to grow vigorously in spring, so do the weeds and moss. This is a busy time in all parts of the garden, but do not neglect the lawn – it needs attention now to prepare for summer.

Summer

Regular cutting is essential throughout summer, but do not cut too short. Heavy wear and tear and drought conditions may take their toll, but you can aid recovery by watering and feeding.

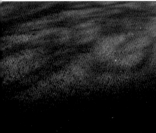

Autumn

Collecting leaves from the lawn is a regular, and important, task. Left alone, moss will start to spread, so treat it before it invades over winter. Feeding and renovating the lawn will reward next season.

Winter

The lawn is lovely to look at in winter and provides the dominant green in the garden when trees are bare and flowers are few. Keep off the grass in frosty conditions to prevent damage.

Lawncare in spring

Spring is the peak of the lawncare season. The grass starts to grow as soon as the temperature rises and the days lengthen. We become more aware of the condition of our lawn because we are out there looking at it at close quarters. Whatever attention a lawn needs, best results will be achieved by a gradual approach, rather than one weekend's onslaught of cutting, raking and applying lawn treatments.

As the early bulbs emerge, so the grass starts to grow.

Now is the last chance to sort out any bumps and dips and changes to the lawn's shape

The first cut of the season Much of the UK now has mild winters and the grass continues to grow for most of the year. If it has been cut periodically through the winter, the first spring cut is not too great an ordeal. If it has been left to grow, the kindest thing – for the lawn, the mower and the gardener – is to reduce its height gradually.

Set the mower on a higher setting than you would normally use: around 5cm (2in). If the grass is long, use an even higher setting: if it is short, you may be able to cut at 4cm (1.5in).

Follow the one-third rule: reduce the length of the grass by only one-third of the total length of the grass blades.

Controlling moss and weeds If moss is a problem, now is the time to apply a moss treatment. If the infestation is heavy, try to get rid of most of the moss before applying a slow-release fertiliser to the lawn. (See pages 30–33.)

If there is only a small amount of moss, you can combine moss control with weeding and feeding. Use a triple-action product (see page 43).

If the lawn is in really poor condition and drastic action is needed, you may need to follow a programme of restoration (see pages 26–29).

Seeding and re-seeding The ideal time to sow grass seed is in spring, while the soil is moist and there is adequate rainfall. This applies whether you are filling in bare patches, oversowing a thin lawn after you have restored its condition, or seeding a new area of lawn. Remember not to sow too thickly; this can cause problems later. Keep newly sown grass seed well watered in dry spells as drought will interfere with germination and the subsequent establishment of the lawn.

Humps and hollows Now is the last chance to sort out any bumps and dips and changes to the lawn's shape before summer. In the days when cylinder mowers were the norm, rolling a lawn used to be standard practice to sort out irregularities. In fact, rolling a lawn causes compaction, impeding drainage and reducing the air space that is so important for healthy grass roots.

Bumps and dips are better sorted individually with a spade. Using a sharp spade, cut into the turf in a straight line across the centre of the bump or dip. At each end of the incision cut at right angles to the first incision, to make a generous H-shaped cut. Carefully slide the spade under the turf at a depth of 3cm (1in) and lift the turf, turning it back on each side from the centre of the bump or dip. This exposes the soil in the middle of the uneven area. Excess soil can then be removed from a bump, or

Getting the lawn in shape in early spring sets off beds and borders as they burst into bloom.

additional fine soil can be added to fill a dip. In both cases, loosen the soil lightly with a hand or digging fork before replacing and firming the turf in position. Firm gently, either by patting down with the back of the spade or by placing a plank of wood over the area and firming with your foot.

Aeration and conditioning All lawns benefit from periodic aeration: on heavy soils, every year or two; on light, well-drained soils, every three years. On the average lawn this is easily achieved by plunging the tines of a garden fork into the turf to a depth of 15cm (6in) or so, roughly every 30cm (12in) across the surface of the lawn. Do this when the ground is soft. For larger areas, a wheeled or mechanical aerator will make the job easier.

Follow this with an application of lawn dressing. (See pages 27–29.)

Lawncare in summer

Summer is the season when the lawn gets most use and is probably under the greatest pressure. The grass grows quickly when the weather is warm and the soil is moist: it needs frequent cutting. Hot, dry weather takes its toll: the lawn starts to turn dry and brown, craving water – which may not be readily available.

Warm weather makes the roses bloom. The grass grows quickly and needs regular cutting.

In drought conditions lawns go dry and brown…there is no need to panic

Mowing Mow the lawn frequently, but not too short. When the grass is growing quickly it is always tempting to cut it as short as possible. However, this puts the grass under great pressure and exposes the brown papery sheaths that cover the stems and new leaves, making the grass appear brown. Leave more of the grass foliage intact and the lawn will look greener.

Watering The lawn sprinkler has always been considered a garden essential. With drier summers and the threat of water shortage, the use of sprinklers may be limited in some areas.

If the use of sprinklers is permitted, choose a good-quality, oscillating model and set it up carefully to water evenly. This may mean moving it around the lawn regularly. Use in the early morning or evening, and not in windy weather. On a hot and sunny, breezy day half the water from a sprinkler will have evaporated before it hits the ground.

Flooding the grass has no advantage; grass roots go deep and will be drawing water from way below the surface. Gentle watering over a long period ensures the water penetrates the soil rather than running off the surface.

Lawn treatments Avoid using slow-release granular lawn fertilisers in hot, dry weather. Granular fertilisers need water to break down the granules. Without it, they remain on the surface and may scorch the grass.

To green-up the grass, use a lawn conditioner. This is applied after the lawn has been cut and delivers a nitrogen boost that will green the grass. This type of fertiliser is formulated as small, light granules and needs minimal moisture to make it effective; early morning dew is usually sufficient. Because the level of nutrients in this type of fertiliser is low, there is no risk of scorching the grass and application is quick and easy.

Lawn weed killers are best applied when the soil is moist and weeds are growing actively. In dry conditions they can cause damage to the grass because the grass blades are softer and cannot easily repel the weedkiller solution. Use a spot lawn weed killer on large, broad-leaved weeds and leave other treatments until after rain has fallen.

In large gardens grass can be left to grow long in informal areas, under trees perhaps.

Dry, brown lawns In drought conditions lawns, especially those consisting of finer grasses, go dry and brown; this may not look attractive but there is no need to panic. In dry conditions lawn grasses do not die; they just go dormant. The living foliage is protected by the brown papery sheaths that cover the base of the leaves, and the grass plants can survive for several weeks without water.

Once it rains, the leaves emerge and the grass quickly greens up. You can then cut the grass lightly to even up the effect. Apply a liquid, soluble or granular fast-acting lawn treatment to boost growth rate and aid recovery.

Wear and tear Where a lawn is used as a play area, temporary damage will inevitably occur. A paddling pool left on the lawn for a week will leave a large, yellow, flattened patch of grass. A goal mouth will soon have a well-worn area in front of it. These damaged and worn areas will recover but it is better, if possible, to move play equipment on a regular basis. This spreads the damaged patches more widely across the lawn, but the damage to any one area is less severe and the grass will recover more quickly.

The ground under and around play equipment always becomes compacted. When you have moved the equipment, water the area thoroughly and spike with a garden fork (see page 27); after a few days apply a fast-acting granular lawn conditioner and water in.

Lawncare in autumn

Autumn is a lovely time of the year in the garden. After the stresses of summer, plants rally with a late crop of flowers; fruits and berries ripen, colourful tints invade the leaf canopy. The lawn responds to cooler temperatures and moister conditions with lush green growth, often moist from dewfall for most of the day. This is an important time for the lawn; care taken now will reap rewards and result in a lawn in better shape for winter and next spring.

Late flowers such as dahlias light up the autumn border. The lawn needs attention now, before winter sets in.

If you are going to feed the grass only once a year, do so in autumn

Cutting Old gardening books recommend cleaning the mower after the last cut of the summer, then storing it away until next spring. With today's milder climate, this no longer applies; grass grows throughout the year and in most places the lawn needs mowing through autumn, even if not quite as frequently as the season progresses.

Collecting leaves As leaves fall from the trees they must be picked up off the lawn. Left lying, they rob the grass of light, and the warm humid conditions underneath the leaves stimulate soft, weak growth that is susceptible to disease.

Rake leaves up regularly, using a flat-tine, plastic lawn rake. This is an efficient, easy-to-use tool, and the leaves do not get impaled on the tines of the rake. A moss rake with spring steel tines is much harder to use and will spear the leaves onto the tines. Use plastic leaf scoops or two short planks of wood to pick up the piles of leaves and transfer them to a barrow or directly into plastic sacks for composting (see pages 54–56).

Leaves can also be collected efficiently with a rotary mower. Set the mower on its highest setting and simply mow up the fallen leaves. This chops the leaves a little and adds a few grass cuttings, which will aid the composting process.

Feeding If you are going to feed the grass only once a year, do so in autumn. Autumn lawn fertiliser contains slow-release nitrogen for green grass and leaf growth, phosphorus (phosphate) to strengthen the grass roots, and potassium (potash), which helps to strengthen the grass leaves, making them more resistant to winter damage. There is nearly always sufficient moisture to break down the granules, so there is no need to worry about watering. If the weather is mild, autumn lawn treatments can be used through to the end of the year.

Moss control The damp, mild weather of autumn and the slower growth of the grass provide the ideal conditions for moss growth. By controlling moss in the autumn you are starting at the root of the problem rather than trying to clear an infestation in spring. The ideal solution is to apply a combined autumn lawn feed and moss killer and rake out the blackened moss after a couple of weeks. Because the infestation should be fairly light at this stage, raking out the moss is not arduous.

Fungi Autumn is a time when mushrooms and toadstools appear in the lawn. These are usually growing on decaying organic matter under the ground, perhaps a piece of dead tree root. They are usually harmless and

Fallen leaves make a colourful carpet. Rake them up regularly to prevent damage to the lawn.

will not damage the grass and can be swept or raked away. Fairy rings are more of a problem but they are not a common sight in most areas (see page 44).

Lawn pests Late summer and autumn are times to tackle the control of lawn pests, particularly leatherjackets and chafer grubs (see page 46). Their presence is indicated by dead patches of grass on the surface of the lawn, particularly evident during late summer when the grass is under stress. The grass dies because the grubs beneath the surface eat the grass roots.

Biological control offers an alternative to chemical treatments. This involves watering a solution of microscopic organisms onto the soil surface; the soil must be adequately warm and moist. Chemical control is also available; the chemical is applied as a drench to the soil surface. Autumn is the ideal time to treat these pests because the larvae are nearest to the surface of the soil at this time. If the attack is severe and sustained, it may be worth consulting a specialist lawn contractor.

Lawncare in winter

The lawn becomes a dominant feature in the winter garden: a large green space whose outline becomes defined as the foliage in beds and borders retreats. Frost transforms the lawn into a crystal carpet, a scene to be enjoyed from the house. Outside, there are leaves and pests to be dealt with and work to be done in preparation for the coming season.

Parchment leaves and faded seedheads are magically transformed by frost. Make sure leaves are not blown onto the grass.

Looking at the lawn The shape of the lawn becomes more obvious in winter, making it a good time to evaluate the lawn as a part of the garden design (see pages 6–9). Keep the edges in trim; this sharpens the lawn's appearance, even if the grass has not been cut.

Remove leaves from the edge of beds and borders; these only blow onto the grass. Either compost them or heap them into the centre of the beds under a generous layer of garden compost or well-rotted manure. Over the course of winter, earthworms will do the work for you by carrying the leaves down into the soil. If you encourage worms to work in the border, you may deter them from too much activity in the lawn.

Avoid walking on the grass when it is frozen; this causes damage to the grass leaves

Avoid walking on the grass when it is frozen; this causes damage to the grass leaves and makes black marks, which persist until the grass grows again.

Wormcasts Wormcasts appear on some lawns in autumn and winter. These may look a bit unsightly but, far from being harmful, they are actually beneficial. Worms aerate the ground for you and deliver top dressing to the surface of the lawn. Wait for a dry spell, then distribute the casts over the surface with a lawn broom or flat-tine, plastic rake.

Collecting leaves The leaves of some deciduous trees, especially oak, can be very late to fall; others blow onto the lawn from borders and corners of the garden. It is important to keep the grass as free of this leaf litter as possible during winter. Grass plants need all the direct light they can get and leaves will only block what little there is when the days are short and the sun is low.

Mowing In mild conditions, and if the ground is firm and the grass dry enough, grass can be cut throughout the winter. Do not cut it too short, or when there is danger of frosty weather. Lightly topping the grass during the winter keeps the lawn in shape and makes it easier to cut in spring, when the grass starts to grow in earnest.

Equipment maintenance Now is an excellent time to get your mower serviced. The unprepared gardener leaves it till spring, then faces a wait of several weeks for the return of his machine at a time when the lawn needs frequent mowing. Servicing in winter means no interruption to the maintenance programme.

Moss, algae and liverwort Moss can be treated and raked out in early winter, but once the weather becomes severe and frosty leave it alone until early spring. Algae and liverwort appear on thin areas of the lawn in shade, usually on poorly drained soil. They are all primitive plants surviving on moisture on the surface. Tackle the cause of the problem: improve drainage conditions by spiking the lawn and adding a top dressing. (See pages 30–33.)

Frosty scenes should be admired from a distance: keep off the lawn, to prevent damage to the grass.

Weeds Weeds seem to grow whatever the season. Lawn weed killers need warm temperatures and high light levels to be most effective but they do work in winter, if much more slowly. Although it is not a good idea to apply a selective lawn weed killer to a large area of the lawn, you can treat individual lawn weeds with a ready-to-use spray. The effectiveness of the weed killer will be slow but it will check the weeds and stop them from spreading. Only do this in a spell of mild weather.

Moles Moles often appear in late winter as they search for earthworms, their principal food. Mounds of soil appear overnight, becoming more numerous by the day and quickly causing devastation to the lawn. Trapping is the only certain remedy (see page 48). Alternatively, consult a professional.

Restoring a lawn

Most of us are faced with the problem of restoring a faded lawn at some time, perhaps after a dry summer, a long cold winter or simply after a few years of neglect. The result is often a patchy lawn, with weeds, lots of moss, coarse weed grasses and liverwort. The temptation is to apply a feed, weed and moss killer, and throw on some extra seed – or, in the worst case scenario, to start again. However, normally the best solution is a programme of restoration that will bring even a sorely neglected lawn back to life.

When is the best time to tackle the job? You can embark on a programme of lawn restoration in either early autumn or early spring. In both cases the soil is moist, so the grass has a chance to grow and recover. However, the ideal time to start the process is autumn. Grass plants are more inclined to produce thickening side shoots in autumn, whereas in spring they produce strong, upright growth. Scarifying a lawn removes moss and debris, enabling the grass plants to produce this thickening growth.

Once the weather turns cold, and the days shorten, growth slows down. Depending on the weather, it may be necessary to delay oversowing with seed until early spring.

Use a spring-tine lawn rake to remove moss and thatch.

Step one: Scarify

Scarifying means dragging out of the lawn any moss and 'thatch'. The latter comprises the partially dead, horizontal rhizomes of grass plants and their decaying leaves, which build up and separate the living grass from the soil. Remove it and you will allow more air, water and light into the young vigorous parts of the grass plants.

● On small lawns you can use a scarifying rake with hooked steel tines or a good-quality moss rake with spring steel tines. It is hard work, and for larger areas it is worth buying or hiring a petrol-driven lawn scarifier with wire tines (see page 31).

If the lawn is lightly infested with patches of moss, kill the moss before you scarify. Apply a moss killer, then wait for a few days before scarifying or you will spread the moss further. If the lawn is heavily infested throughout, scarify first, kill the moss, then scarify again if necessary.

Step two: Aerate

When the soil beneath a lawn becomes compacted, the amount of air space between the soil particles is reduced. This eventually interferes with the healthy growth of the grass plants. Aeration involves making holes in the lawn to a depth of 10–15cm (4–6in). These holes allow air and water to get down to the grass roots. If you apply a lawn dressing after aeration, some of the dressing will fill the holes, getting fresh, loose soil to where the lawn needs it.

The best tool is a hollow-tine lawn aerator, which removes plugs of soil from the ground. However, in reality they are not often used because they are hard work and are only successful on soil that is easy to penetrate. They are virtually impossible to use on stony soils and heavy, dry soils. They must always be used when the soil is moist.

A garden fork is the next best thing. Plunge it deep and open the holes left by the tines by pushing the fork back and forth. It is hard work, so do it while the ground is soft. A good-quality, stainless steel digging fork is ideal; the polished tines penetrate the ground easily and are easy to remove.

There is no need to aerate the whole lawn at once. Divide large areas into manageable portions and do one bit a day over a week or so.

Step three: Restore

Once you have scarified the lawn and spiked it all over with a fork, it is time to apply a lawn dressing.

Moss survives drought! Moss is usually considered a problem in the cool, damp conditions of autumn and winter, but it does seem to survive drought and recovers quickly when moist conditions return. A parched brown lawn often reveals yellowish-green patches of moss lurking beneath the grass; these soon start to grow again in late summer, hindering the recovery of the grass. A heavy infestation of moss in a dry lawn acts as a sponge, absorbing water before it can penetrate through to the grass roots. In these conditions it is better to rake out the moss prior to applying a moss killer. The sooner the moss is removed, the sooner the grass will begin to recover.

Use a fork to aerate the lawn when the soil is moist.

Above: Tip the lawn dressing into a barrow and loosen with a fork before spreading. Below: Use a plasic rake or broom to spread the dressing evenly over the lawn.

● Lawn dressing is a mixture of fine, sieved loam, an organic soil conditioner (often peat) and sand – the magic ingredient that will improve drainage and aeration. It is a bulky product and never goes as far as you think; a pile of bags quickly disappears, even on a moderately sized lawn. Tip the dressing into a wheelbarrow, loosen it up with a garden fork to separate the particles, then distribute it by casting it across the lawn with a spade. A 25-litre bag will cover about 10–12sq m (12–14sq yd).

● Some lawn dressings contain a slow-release fertiliser, but if this is not the case you can add a modest amount of a general lawn fertiliser (without weed killer or moss killer) to the dressing before applying it. Work out the area that a bag of lawn dressing will cover and add the corresponding amount of fertiliser according to the manufacturer's instructions. If you do this, or use a lawn dressing containing fertiliser, make sure distribution is even across the area of the lawn or you will get a patchy effect when the fertiliser becomes active.

● Work the lawn dressing lightly into the surface of the lawn using a broom or a plastic-tine rake. Free the grass blades without damaging them, ensuring that the dressing is spread evenly and the grass blades are not buried. The back of an ordinary garden rake is a useful tool to run over the lawn, after distribution, to make sure that no bumps or dips have been created.

● A generous application of lawn dressing makes the lawn unsightly at first but the grass will soon respond and grow quickly. After two or three weeks it will be hard to remember just how thin and unattractive the lawn looked for a few days.

● Professional green-keepers apply lawn dressing every autumn. This may not be necessary in the garden, but aim to do it every two or three years.

Three weeks or so later...

If the first two steps have left the grass really thin or very patchy, oversow now with a quality lawn seed. On fine lawns, use a rye-free seed mixture; on hard-wearing ones, use a seed mix containing dwarf perennial ryegrass. If you began the restoration process in autumn, leave this until spring, when the weather is warmer.

● Oversow lightly. Adding more grass seed than recommended will not give better results; it will simply result in overcrowded grass plants. Sow bare patches and lightly cover the seed with lawn dressing. This provides the ideal growing conditions for young grass plants.

● Once the grass seed has germinated and is growing strongly, it is time to apply a slow-release lawn fertiliser, which will feed and strengthen the grass through the growing season. This can be a combined product containing weed killer and/or moss killer but care should be taken if new grass seed has recently been sown.

● If this is the case it is better to use a fertiliser and spot treat any weeds with a selective lawn weed killer. Remember that annual weeds that emerge in any bare patches will be removed by mowing.

Restoring areas damaged by heavy wear and tear Many lawns have areas that are subject to more wear and tear: perhaps a main thoroughfare, a goal mouth, the swingball area, the garden cricket pitch. Heavy use will cause soil compaction, so aeration and the application of lawn dressing will be particularly beneficial on an annual basis.

Any weeds that appear are easily treated with a ready-to-use lawn weed killer.

Aim to apply lawn dressing every two to three years

Controlling moss

Moss is a problem in most lawns, encouraged by mild, damp weather in autumn and early winter. If moss gets a hold at the end of the year and is left unchecked, it will be very invasive by spring. Algae and liverwort thrive in similar conditions, and coarse weed grasses are ready to invade and spoil the appearance of the lawn.

Moss – what is it?

Moss is a primitive plant with very fine leaves and stems that need moisture to avoid desiccation. It also needs water around it to reproduce, as it does not produce flowers and seeds. It can grow in conditions of low fertility and it loves the humid, protected environment provided by a colony of short grass plants: the lawn.

How fussy should I be about moss? Moss in a lawn is not unattractive.
It often stays greener than grass in drought. However, it is not the same green as grass and if you want an emerald sward, you do not want moss.

Moss competes with grass and if left unchecked will build up and weaken the grass. Eventually it creates a soft and springy carpet with a few fine blades of grass sticking out through the moss. When lawns get to this stage, renovation is necessary (see pages 26–29). For this reason, early and regular treatment is essential.

Moss grows prolifically in the moist conditions between the grass blades.

How can I prevent moss?

As with weeds, moss infestation can be reduced by effective lawn care. Good growing conditions for moss are usually poor growing conditions for grass. Healthy grass competes with moss and reduces its spread.

● Moss likes moisture, particularly on the soil surface. Improved drainage means poorer growing conditions for moss and better conditions for grass. Aerate the lawn by spiking (see page 27).

● Catch moss infestations early. Rake out patches of moss and treat them as they appear, rather than letting them spread.

● Keep grass growing vigorously by feeding and dressing the lawn regularly.

● Avoid build-up of thatch, the dead material that collects between the green foliage of the lawn and the soil surface. Maintain air circulation by raking and scarifying the lawn regularly.

● If moss is not killed off in autumn, it will continue to grow through the winter. Apply an autumn lawn feed that incorporates moss killer.

How can I get rid of moss?

There are several ways to control moss in lawns. Usually a chemical treatment is used in combination with raking or mechanical removal.

Manual raking A good-quality lawn rake with spring steel tines can be used to rake moss out of a lawn; this is the traditional method of control. If you do this in the early stages and the moss has already been killed, raking is very effective. If moss has not been killed first, raking can spread the moss to other areas of the lawn. Using a rake on a large area is hard work.

Moss can be raked out with a spring-tine lawn rake.

Mechanical moss rakes Electric and petrol-driven rakes are available that make light work of large areas. Electric machines are ideal for small and medium-sized lawns. For large areas it may be worth hiring a machine with a petrol-driven engine. Some cultivators come with spring-tine attachments that can be used as moss and thatch rakes for lawns.

Moss killers Nearly all moss killers are based on iron sulphate (ferrous sulphate). When they are applied, either as a solution or in a solid formulation, moss quickly turns black and dies. Grass also looks black after application, but as the grass leaves are tougher than the moss, the grass is unharmed whereas the moss dies.

Liquid formulations Liquid moss killers are usually iron sulphate in solution. These are supplied either as a concentrate, for dilution, or as a solid that dissolves in water. The solution is applied with a watering can or sprayer. A sprayer is more economical but, because of the dense nature of a moss colony, you must be sure to wet the moss sufficiently for the solution to take effect. If you use a sprayer, adjust the nozzle to produce a coarse spray. After treatment, the dead moss must be raked out after about two weeks. Left in situ, it will still rob the grass of light and air.

Combined fertilisers and moss killers Moss killers are often applied as a combined formulation with a fertiliser, or with fertiliser and weed killer as a triple-action treatment.

Autumn lawn fertilisers and moss killers remove the moss before it becomes more established over winter

There are formulations specifically for autumn use and others for spring and summer use (see pages 42–43). They should be applied when the soil is moist and the grass is dry. If rain does not fall within a day or two, you must water, to activate the product and to wash it onto the grass and moss, and into the soil.

Some formulations are coarse powders; others are granular. Even distribution is necessary, and a spreader is best used on larger areas. Leave for two weeks after application before raking out the moss – this allows time for the fertiliser to be dissolved into the soil water. If the moss is removed too quickly, it will probably take some of the solid fertiliser granules with it, reducing the effectiveness of the product.

Autumn lawn fertilisers and moss killers are particularly effective because they remove the moss before it becomes more established over winter.

Lawn sand Lawn sand is a traditional treatment for moss control. It consists of iron (ferrous) sulphate mixed with sand and sulphate of ammonia (the latter supplies nitrogen to green the grass). Although effective, it is not easy to apply. It has a corrosive action and tends to block lawn spreaders or to pour through them too quickly, resulting in over-application. Lawn sand can easily cause damage to a lawn if used carelessly.

What else should I watch out for?

In addition to moss, there are other plants – apart from weeds (see pages 34–38) – that can be a problem.

Warning… Iron sulphate turns moss black almost immediately. It also blackens weeds temporarily and it stains paving. After the solution has been applied and is still wet, take great care not to walk on the grass and then into the house. Do try not to get the solution on clothing: stains are virtually impossible to remove.

Algae and liverwort

Algae and liverwort are also primitive plants, enjoying similar conditions to moss, and are common problems in lawns. They mainly appear in late autumn and early winter in shady areas where the ground is compacted and drainage is poor.

A moss-free lawn is bright emerald green in colour.

Algae appear as a green slime on the soil surface between the grass plants. In extreme conditions they become a gelatinous, bubbly green mass. Liverwort is more sophisticated in its growth habit, producing flattened seaweed-like 'leaves' of dark green, slimy when wet. These grow flat on the soil surface and compete successfully with weak grass.

Moss killers give some control but the key to success is to improve the drainage and apply a lawn dressing with extra sharp sand. This will improve the growing conditions and increase the drainage at the soil surface.

Both algae and liverwort are more unsightly than they are harmful and are relatively easy to eradicate.

Weed grasses

Undesirable weed grasses eventually appear in most lawns. Annual meadow grass, with coarse, light green leaves and greyish flowers, shows up easily among fine, emerald green grasses. Woodrush, a dwarf sedge with pointed leaves in silvery tufts and brown flowerheads in spring, is a problem on sandy, acid soils.

These weed 'grasses' are virtually impossible to eradicate using chemicals because their foliage is so similar to that of the grasses. The only answer is to keep an eye open for them and dig them out as they appear.

Coarse grasses form light-coloured, unsightly clumps in the lawn.

Once a lawn is overrun by weed grasses, if you want a fine, traditional lawn there is no alternative but to start again. In a more rustic setting, coarser weed grasses may be perfectly acceptable in the lawn.

Controlling weeds

Weeds appear in all lawns at some time. Seeds are blown in on the breeze, are carried in by birds and animals, and are already present in the soil. Some creeping weeds spread from neighbouring paths and flower borders. Any thin patches in the grass present the perfect opportunity for weeds to invade and get a hold.

Top: Plantain. Above: White clover with buttercups.

Feeding the lawn regularly puts it in better shape to compete with weeds and moss

How fussy should I be?

That depends on the lawn. A fine, manicured lawn is more easily disfigured by weeds than a lawn of coarser grasses in an informal setting. For example, a lawn in a rural situation may be completely overrun with clover and still look attractive. In small fine lawns, weeds are easy to spot and therefore easier to treat at an early stage.

Different types of lawn weed

There are many different lawn weeds, but essentially they fall into two main categories:

Rosette-forming weeds These form broad, flat rosettes of leaves. They compete with the grass by flattening their leaves as the plants develop, pushing the surrounding grass blades down and away as they grow. They have relatively large leaves, are easy to spot in the lawn and are fairly easily treated.

Examples: plantain, catsear, dandelion, daisy, buttercup.

Mat-forming weeds These usually have creeping stems that weave between the grass plants, gradually forming broad mats of plantlets in the lawn. They normally have small leaves and compete with the grass by pushing up between the grass plants, robbing them of light, water and nutrients. They are not easy to spot when young and are more difficult to eradicate.

Examples: white clover, speedwell, yarrow, selfheal.

How can I prevent weeds in my lawn?

Weeds need an opportunity to establish in the lawn. Prevent the opportunity from occurring and you reduce the number of weeds. Weeds usually invade when the grass is thin and there are bare patches. These are the defensive measures to take:

● Avoid cutting the grass too short: close-cropped lawns mean weaker grass, that is grass that is less able to compete with germinating weed seedlings.

● Do not let the lawn become overrun by moss in winter. Killing moss in spring leaves bare patches after the dead moss has been raked out – an ideal opportunity for weeds to establish.

● Watch out for weeds after drought. When the lawn has dried out in summer, bare earth is exposed between the grass plants. Weed seeds are abundant in the air and will blow in on the breeze. As the grass starts to grow, so do the weeds. It may be necessary to apply a selective weedkiller at this time.

● Feed the lawn regularly in spring and autumn. This strengthens the grass, putting it in better shape to compete with weeds and moss.

How can I get rid of weeds?

There are several ways to get rid of weeds in a lawn but on large areas lawn weed killers are probably the most practical solution.

From the top: Catsear, dandelion, selfheal, daisies,

Digging out Large individual weeds can be dug out of the turf with a narrow trowel, lawn knife or daisy grubber. A few daisies or plantains are easily dealt with in this way. When removing dandelions, thistles and deep-rooted perennial weeds, make sure all of the roots are removed; any fragments will regenerate.

Raking Some creeping weeds, such as clover and speedwell, can be controlled to a certain extent by raking. A spring-tined lawn rake will lift the rhizomes to the surface of the lawn, where any that are not dragged out will be cut back by

the mower. This is never a complete solution, but it may reduce the population to a number that can be tackled effectively with a weed killer.

A lawn weed killer, applied in solution using a large sprayer, is the best way to control weeds on a big lawn.

Mowing Mowing wipes out many annual weeds and weakens strong upright weeds such as thistles and nettles to the point where they cannot survive. Mowing is particularly effective in new lawns: a large population of weeds often emerges in a new lawn but it usually disappears after a few mowings.

Selective lawn weed killers Selective lawn weed killers are the principal method of weed control in lawns. These attack the weeds but, if used properly, leave the grass unharmed.

Lawn weed killers – how do they work?

Most grass blades grow vertically, are narrow and have a waxy outer layer that repels water. On a lawn wet with rain or dew, water droplets hang on to the grass blades and do not wet the surface of the leaves. Lawn weeds have broader leaves, which often lie horizontally, so they are easier to wet. When a solution of lawn weed killer is applied, it rolls off the grass but sticks to many of the weed leaves. From here it is absorbed into the plants, affecting the growth hormones and eventually killing the plants. Weeds with larger leaves are the most quickly affected: their leaves grow above the grass and distort when the weed killer is applied. They are then eliminated by mowing, and the roots wither away.

Weed killers do not have such a strong impact on weeds with small leaves; these react more slowly because they absorb less of the weed killer. More difficult weeds, such as speedwell, clover, yarrow and oxalis, may need further applications at two- to three-week intervals to bring them under control.

When should I apply lawn weed killer?

Weed control is most effective when the weeds and grass are growing actively, from mid-spring on. Ideally, cut the lawn, wait a few days until the weeds and grass have started to grow again, then apply the weed killer.

● Do not apply weed killer if the ground is very dry or the weather is hot and sunny. Choose a still day, when rain is not expected as a shower after application will dilute the chemical and reduce its effect.

How do I apply lawn weed killer?

Lawn weed killers can be applied in three main ways. They are available ready-mixed in a sprayer; as a concentrate for dilution with water; and combined with lawn feed (fertilizer) or lawn feed and moss killer.

Ready-to-use sprays Handy ready-to-use sprays are convenient and easy to use. The weed killer is ready-mixed with water in the sprayer, so it is just a matter of directing the nozzle at the weeds and spraying. Droplet size is large, so there is little chance of the spray drifting onto surrounding planting. Some ready-to-use weed killers have a foaming action, so it is easy to see where

Warning… Take care that the weed killer you are using is a lawn weed killer and not a general weed killer. The latter kills grass as well as weeds! It is surprising how often lawns are wiped out just because instructions on the bottle or packet were not read carefully before the product was used.

Lawn weed killers will damage all other broad-leaved plants so be careful to avoid the foliage of plants in beds and borders. Do not use in windy weather.

Note… Many gardeners do not like the idea of handling chemicals. Wear gloves and adequate protective clothing and wash your hands after use as a precaution. Wash out the watering can or sprayer after use. Ideally have a dedicated can or sprayer for weed killers to prevent any potential damage to precious plants.

Black medick.

Remember... You do not have to apply lawn weed killer concentrates over the whole area of the lawn. Use it only where there are weeds. Alternatively, if weeds are widespread in the lawn, you could combine the weed killer with a soluble or liquid lawn fertilizer (diluted in the same volume of water) and treat the whole lawn. This will give the grass a boost, at the same time as killing the weeds.

the spray has been used. The foam holds the chemical on the leaves while it is absorbed.

This is the ideal way to treat a few individual weeds and to tackle new weeds as they appear. It is an expensive method of weed control on a big lawn and is tedious and time-consuming on large areas.

Concentrates These are diluted with water and are applied to the lawn with a watering can or pressure sprayer. A knapsack sprayer is ideal for larger lawns. When the concentrate is to be applied with a sprayer, it is diluted in a smaller volume of water than when it is to be applied in a watering can; this is a more economical and effective method of application.

A coarse spray should be used to avoid drift, and ideally there should be a hood over the nozzle of the sprayer, which is held close to the ground.

● Follow the instructions on dilution closely; there is no advantage in using more of the chemical than recommended by the manufacturer.

Combined products Many lawn fertilizers contain a weed killer and some incorporate a moss killer as well. These dual- or triple-action products save time and effort by reducing the number of operations and eliminating the need for mixing and spraying weed killers. Combined products are useful for initial treatment of weeds but usually a follow-up spot treatment is required to eliminate difficult weeds.

● Combined lawn feed, weed killer and moss killer needs careful application to avoid scorch and to achieve even results (see page 42).

● To achieve maximum weed control, apply the product in mid-spring, when grass and weeds are growing actively and the soil is moist.

● You must be able to water the lawn following application if rain does not fall within 48 hours.

Lawn fertilisers

There is a great variety of lawn fertilisers to choose from, in liquid, soluble and granular form. Some may at first appear better value than others, but contents vary greatly. Some supply fewer nutrients than others but in a faster-acting form; others supply more nutrients and release them over a long period. All have their uses, but it is important to choose the right product if you are to achieve the result you are hoping for.

Why should I feed the lawn?

Of course, feeding the lawn stimulates growth, which means you will have to cut it more! However, without feeding, few lawns retain their colour and quality over the years. A weaker lawn is more susceptible to moss, weeds and disease, all of which require time and effort to deal with them.

Regular feeding greens the grass and keeps the lawn in good condition.

Remember that a lawn is a dense plantation, with each plant competing for light, air, water and nutrients. You need to provide additional plant food to fulfil the needs of each grass plant.

When growth is lush and rapid, try to cut the lawn regularly. This is good for the grass and means cutting is less of a chore.

What are the main nutrients a lawn needs?

There are three major nutrients required by all plants for growth and development:

● NITROGEN (N) is needed for leaf and stem growth. As grass is grown for its leaves, this is particularly important for lawns.

● PHOSPHORUS (P), usually referred to as phosphate, is required for strong, healthy root development. Any plant is only ever as good as its roots, and this goes for grass as well.

● POTASSIUM (K), or potash, is mainly needed for flowers and fruit. Potassium also helps to toughen up plants and promote hardiness. This is particularly important for lawn grasses in winter.

The content of any fertiliser is represented on the packet by the NPK ratio. For example, a fertiliser with an NPK ratio of 4:0:0 has 4 per cent nitrogen and no phosphorus or potassium, whereas a fertiliser with a ratio of 12:2:4 has 12 per cent nitrogen, 2 per cent phosphorus and 4 per cent potassium.

Granular fertilisers can be distributed with a hand-held spreader – ideal for small areas.

What types of fertiliser are there?

Fertilisers can be applied in either liquid or solid form. The various types of fertiliser do different jobs. The means of application is a matter of personal preference.

Liquid and soluble fertilisers These are applied in the main growing season and are fast-acting. Because the nutrients are applied in solution, they become available to the grass roots as soon as they are carried down into the soil. They are a source of nitrogen, so they stimulate growth.

They can be applied using a watering can, a sprayer adjusted to produce a coarse spray, or a hose-end diluter. The latter is the easiest means of application on anything but a very small lawn. On large lawns, a tank sprayer mounted on a ride-on mower is another option.

The effect of liquid and soluble fertilisers is relatively short-lived. As the nutrients are in soluble form, they are easily washed from the soil by rainfall or irrigation.

Granular fertilisers Most gardeners prefer to use granular fertilisers. The nutrients are combined with a carrier that releases them gradually in the presence of soil moisture. Most are slow to release their nutrients. Controlled-release granular fertilisers have coated granules that release nutrients only when the soil is moist and the temperature is warm enough. Release is steady and gradual.

Liquid and soluble lawn fertilisers can be applied with a watering can, and may be combined with lawn weed killer.

Fast-acting granular fertilisers These supply a relatively small amount of nutrient, usually only nitrogen. They can be used regularly during the growing season to green-up the grass and maintain its appearance. They are applied after mowing and can be used when conditions are relatively dry. As long as there is some rainfall or heavy dew, they will work and will not harm the lawn. There is little risk of scorch or damage caused by uneven application.

Slow-acting granular fertilisers These contain a larger amount of nutrients and are released slowly over a long period. Often the nitrogen is in two forms – one for immediate use, the other released over a period of several weeks. Even application is important to avoid a patchy effect.

Hand-held applicators are useful on small areas, while a wheeled lawn spreader is virtually essential on medium-sized to large lawns.

Set the lawn spreader to the correct setting for the product and, with the lever in the off position, carefully fill with fertiliser.

Why do I need one fertiliser for spring and summer and another for autumn?

How to use a granular fertiliser

Take care when applying a granular fertiliser. Plan how you are going to apply it.

● Mark out the lawn, using pegs and coloured twine. Uneven and excessive application can result in scorched areas and a patchy lawn.

● Practise the application first, using an area covered with sheets of newspaper or polythene.

● Applying more fertiliser than recommended does not give better results. At best it is wasteful; at worst it causes damage.

● Apply when the grass is dry and when the soil is moist and rain is expected within 48 hours.

● Lawn spreaders are often made for specific brands of fertilisers. Granule sizes also vary from one brand to another. Make sure you use the right spreader, and that it is set correctly, for the fertiliser you are using. Manufacturers' websites are an excellent source of information: check the product packaging for details.

● If you are using a spreader that does not have an on/off lever, practise turning at the end of the lawn without over-applying the product. If you are not careful, you will scorch the ends of the lawn.

When should I treat the lawn?

Fertilisers are formulated to provide the correct nutrient requirements for the lawn at each particular season.

● Spring and summer fertilisers contain mainly nitrogen, to promote lush green growth, along with some phosphorus and potassium.

● Autumn fertilisers contain some slow-release nitrogen but have larger quantities of phosphorus, for root growth, and potassium, to toughen up the lawn in preparation for cold winter weather.

42

Dual- and triple-action products

A lawn fertiliser is often combined with a weed killer and/or a moss killer. The triple-action feed, weed and moss killer has become the most popular spring and summer lawn treatment. It is appealing in that all treatments are combined in one application. It is ideal for early season use on the regularly maintained lawn that has some moss and some weeds (see page 18). A combined product is unnecessary on a lawn that has no moss or weeds.

● Combined products rarely give total weed control on their own. It may be necessary to follow up with a selective lawn weed killer later in the season.

● If a triple-action lawn feed, weed and moss killer is used in early spring, a lawn fertiliser can be used 6–8 weeks later.

● Autumn lawn fertilisers often incorporate moss killers. They do not contain weed killers because these would not be effective in the colder, shorter days at the end of the year.

What is lawn sand?

Lawn sand is a traditional product still favoured by many gardeners. It consists of horticultural sand blended with iron sulphate, to kill moss, and sulphate of ammonia, to provide nitrogen to green the lawn. The sand improves drainage on heavy soils. It is a difficult product to distribute evenly and if used carelessly can scorch the lawn, producing patchy results. Few lawn spreaders distribute it satisfactorily, as it tends to clog up the holes and corrode metal parts.

It is possible to mix your own lawn sand but this is rarely worthwhile, as it is usually inexpensive to buy.

Lawn sand is not a complete feed and has been largely superseded by modern granular fertilisers and moss killers.

Applying a lawn dressing every two or three years improves the condition of the soil underneath the grass.

Lawn dressings Lawn dressings are applied in early autumn or early spring. They are bulky products, usually a blend of fine loam, sand and an organic soil conditioner (traditionally peat). A slow-release fertiliser is normally incorporated to nourish the lawn. If used regularly, lawn dressings improve the soil beneath the turf, benefiting the lawn in the long term. They are used by professional green-keepers and are an excellent choice to restore neglected and stressed lawns (see pages 27–29).

Pests & diseases

Grasses, like any other plants in the garden, may be susceptible to attack by pests and diseases at some point. As with any other living thing, resistance to disease is greater when plants are growing well, so a healthy, well-cared for lawn is less disease-prone. However, even the best lawns are open to attack by pests of all descriptions.

Mushrooms and toadstools

Fungi in the form of mushrooms and toadstools are common in lawns and usually appear in autumn. They live on decaying woody plant remains, such as old tree roots; the presence of these in the soil will encourage them.

Most fungi are quite harmless and can be left alone. Alternatively, they can be brushed away with a lawn broom or lawn rake. A recurring patch of toadstools can usually be eradicated more permanently by lifting the turf and removing the decaying woody material that supports it.

Fairy rings Some toadstools grow in a ring on the lawn. This ring varies in size from 1m (3ft) in diameter to several metres/feet, and it may get larger from one autumn to the next. In some cases this has no effect on the grass and there is no need to worry. In other cases the grass in the middle of the ring becomes darker and lusher; field mushrooms can cause this effect. Curing the problem is difficult, so the best solution is to feed the lawn in early autumn; this greens the whole lawn, making the ring less visible.

The worst type of fairy ring is a more serious problem. Two darker green rings appear in the turf, one 30cm (12in) or so inside the other. The area between the two rings is discoloured yellow-brown and often fills with moss after a few weeks. The toadstools appear around the outer ring. Smaller than field mushrooms, they are creamy-brown in colour.

There is no easy way to get rid of this problem. It is worth trying a drench of iron sulphate, but if this does not work the only solution is to dig out the whole of the affected area to a depth of 30cm (12in) and to a distance of 30cm (12in) beyond the outer circle. Remove all soil from that part of the lawn and deposit it elsewhere in the garden. Fill the hole with new soil and then seed or re-turf the area.

Fungal diseases

Lawn diseases are not something the gardener should worry about unduly. Look too carefully and you may end up diagnosing a patch of fertiliser damage, or the gaps left by moss or weed treatment, as something more sinister.

Mushrooms and toadstools often appear in lawns in autumn. Most are harmless and do not damage the grass.

The most frequently encountered lawn diseases are:

Snow mould (Fusarium patch)
This is a common disease in autumn and early spring. Small patches of grass turn yellow and spread to leave large brown patches on the lawn. In the mornings and on damp days these appear white and fluffy around the edges. There is no effective treatment available to the amateur. Avoid high-nitrogen fertilisers in autumn. Keep off the grass in frosty weather; this causes damage, which then leaves the lawn susceptible to disease.

Red thread (Corticum disease)
This only affects fine grasses. Patches of bleached grass appear in late summer and autumn. These have a pinkish hue, caused by fine, pin-like red growths on the grass leaves. The patches recover in spring, so the problem is not too serious. Weak, undernourished lawns are susceptible, so feed the grass regularly, spike the lawn and apply a lawn dressing every couple of years.

Dollar spot
This is another disease of fine lawns. Patches are yellow-brown and around 5cm (2in) in diameter. They spread and join up to make larger areas and can severely disfigure the lawn. Good lawn care is the answer.

In all cases, if a disease problem cannot be remedied it is worth consulting a professional lawncare contractor, who may have access to other remedies not available to the amateur gardener.

Lawn pests

The two main pests that cause problems in lawns are leatherjackets and chafer grubs – larvae that feed on the grass roots, causing damage to, or even the death of, the grass plants. Other pests do not feed on the grass but do damage to the lawn by disturbing the soil, by burrowing under the lawn or by scraping, scratching or wearing away the surface.

Leatherjackets

Leatherjackets are the larvae of crane flies or daddy long-legs. The grey-brown grubs are 3–4cm (1–1.5in) long, without legs or visible heads. They feed on the grass roots through spring and summer, causing yellowing or dead brown patches when the lawn is under stress in summer.

There are three methods of control:

● Lay a sheet of black polythene over the lawn overnight in summer. The grubs come to the surface and when the grass is uncovered in the morning can be swept away or left for the birds to eat.

● Use a biological control in late summer or early autumn. Use a watering can to apply a drench of a solution that contains microscopic parasitic worms. These attack and destroy the leatherjackets.

● Use a chemical drench at about the same time of year as biological control.

Top: Crane flies appear early in autumn – their larvae, leatherjackets, feed on grass roots. Above: Chafer grubs, the larval stage of chafer beetles, do similar damage.

Chafer grubs

These grubs are the larvae of chafer beetles. They are fat and cream-coloured with brown heads and blackish tails. These are nearest to the surface of the lawn in late summer, before they burrow deeper during the winter. Late summer is the time to treat them with biological or chemical control in the same way as leatherjackets. Evidence of chafer grub attack is similar to that of leatherjackets. Chafer grubs are common on sandy soil and on grass that was formerly pasture or paddock.

Both these larval pests are responsible for further damage to the lawn when birds, badgers, foxes and other animals search for the larvae in the turf. This damage can be more devastating than that caused by larvae eating the grass roots.

Ants Ants are a summer problem on light sandy soils. Their activity brings fine soil to the surface; this becomes more obvious when the grass is cut. Ants do little physical damage to the grass plants but can disfigure the lawn. If treatment is necessary, liquid ant killers and baits are the best solution; powders look more unsightly than the ant damage.

Mining bees Small mounds of soil appearing on the lawn surface in spring like tiny conical volcanoes with a hole down through the middle indicate the presence of mining bees. They make their home beneath the turf but they do not sting and are quite harmless, so leave them alone. They are most common on light sandy soils, and the mounds soon disappear as the season progresses.

Birds Birds may damage a lawn if there are grubs, worms or ants present. Starlings, crows and green woodpeckers make substantial conical holes in the lawn in search of food. The only way to deter them is to reduce the food source.

Bird-scarers such as a humming line or CDs on wires are an effective way to protect newly sown grass seed.

Earthworms Worms used to be considered a lawn pest and were often eradicated using chemical treatments. These are no longer available to the amateur gardener so earthworm activity, where it occurs, has to be managed rather than prevented or eradicated. Earthworms do not physically attack the grass, but in the spring and autumn they leave mounds of fine, wet soil on the surface of the lawn. When these are numerous, they can be unsightly and cause damage to the turf if they are trodden into the grass or flattened by mowing. They should be dispersed, ideally when fairly dry, over the lawn surface using a lawn broom or plastic lawn rake. Worms are most frequently a problem on heavy, fertile soils in spring and autumn. During this time their presence can attract moles, a much more serious pest (see page 48).

Top: Ants are a common problem on lawns in summer; their activity brings soil to the surface of the lawn. Above: Birds damage the lawn in their search for worms, grubs and ants.

CDs on wires are an effective way to protect newly sown grass seed

Moles, rabbits and badgers
These may be less common pests, but they can certainly cause damage.

Always use gloves when handling and setting traps

Moles Moles cause more rapid damage to a lawn than any other pest. Mounds of soil erupt overnight, becoming more numerous each day as the mole increases his territory in search of food. The extent of the damage leads any gardener to believe that an army of moles must have invaded; in fact it is probably just a single mole.

Various electronic and chemical deterrents are available and many alternative remedies exist, from moth balls to musical greeting cards. Sadly, trapping is the only effective method of eradication.

Humane tunnel traps catch the mole without harming it, so it can be released elsewhere. These must be checked very regularly to ensure speedy release. Whether you use these or conventional traps, some skill and patience are needed.

A molehill means a mole is active and there are more hills to come!

● Always use gloves when handling and setting traps. Old gloves that have been in contact with soil are ideal as any foreign or human scent will have been removed.

● Position traps in a tunnel between recent molehills, never under a hill.

● Ensure that no light, debris or grass from the surface gets into the tunnel, and remove stones.

● Check daily.

Rabbits Rabbits cause damage by shallow burrowing into the soil surface in search of roots and minerals. Damage is most noticeable in late winter and spring before the grass really gets growing. The only solution is to keep the pests out of the area or cull them.

Badgers They do not attack often but when they do, damage is severe. Badgers rip up the lawn surface in search of chafer grubs and ants, so damage is caused where these are prevalent. Control the food source (see pages 46–47) to deter the badgers. Strong wire fencing is needed to keep them out of the garden but it may be worth the investment if all else fails.

Dogs Most dogs are responsible for some lawn damage, particularly as young animals. Scratching, playing and using the lawn as a lavatory all take their toll. Bitches cause the most damage – their urine scorches the grass, leaving yellow and brown patches that take weeks to recover.

Children – and dogs – can impose heavy wear and tear on the confined area of a lawn.

You can reduce the extent of the damage by drenching the patches with water immediately. Alternatively, add tomato pulp or juice to the dog's dry food. In many cases this seems to be a magical solution, neutralising the effect of the urine and rendering it almost harmless to the grass.

Two-legged pests! At certain times of the year the human occupants will cause just as much damage to the lawn as any other pests. Children's play, especially ball games, can cause severe damage to areas of the lawn (see page 21). Garden maintenance tasks done when the lawn is frozen in winter or wet in autumn can cause similar damage (see page 24). However, any lawn is there to be used as well as looked at, and grasses are resilient plants that will usually recover given a little care and attention.

Mowing the lawn

However well you look after your lawn, it is the way you mow it that determines its final appearance. The range of mowing machines available nowadays caters for every type of garden – and gardener. In addition to a mower, there a few other pieces of equipment that are essential for keeping your lawn looking good.

Choosing the right mower

Most gardeners aspire to an evenly cut emerald sward with stripes. At one time this was achieved using a cylinder mower, which has a rotating drum of blades that cut against one fixed blade in a scissor-like action. It is the type of mowing machine used on bowling greens, golf greens and tennis courts. Cylinder mowers need regular maintenance and blade sharpening. Today most lawns are cut with rotary mowers, which have one or two fast-rotating blades that spin horizontally. These are more forgiving of irregularities in the lawn surface, more robust, and easier to use and maintain.

Power-driven machines, fuelled by electricity or petrol, are the natural choice. Very few gardeners use push mowers nowadays.

Warning... Avoid cheap second-hand electric mowers purchased from unreliable sources. A new appliance will have been tested and will comply with current legislation covering the use of electricity in the garden. This may not be the case with a second-hand machine, and its safety cannot be guaranteed. It is not worth the risk.

● Budget electric mowers, usually powered by a brush motor – a simple, inexpensive power source – are available at very low prices. However, you get what you pay for. These are considered disposable items and not repairable, with a working life of about 40 hours.

● A better-quality electric mower will be powered by an induction motor – a more sophisticated and reliable piece of equipment. It will be more expensive but may well be a cost-effective solution in the long term, with a working life of three to ten years.

● All petrol-driven mowers now have four-stroke engines, and run off ordinary unleaded petrol. Gone are the days of mixing two-stroke oil and petrol, worrying whether the mixture is too rich or too weak. And with a petrol mower there is no need for trailing electric cables.

● Always choose a machine that is large and robust enough for the job, not one that is of the bare minimum specification. The larger and more powerful the mower is, the more quickly and effectively it will cut the lawn. Because it does not have to work as hard as a smaller, less powerful machine, it will have a longer life. Also consider manoeuvrability: a large mower may not be easy to use in restricted spaces and on tight corners.

A petrol mower makes light work of mowing, especially if the lawn is cut regularly.

● For all but the smallest gardens, choose a self-propelled mower. In cheaper electric and petrol mowers, the power source drives the blades but you have to push the mower. In self-propelled machines, the power assists the movement of the machine as well as driving the blades. This makes life much easier on large lawns, uneven or sloping ground, and when you are cutting longer grass.

How do I achieve a lawn with stripes?

On a domestic lawn, with developments in technology and engineering, a modern rotary mower can give as good a finish as a cylinder mower. If you choose a good-quality rotary mower with a roller, you will have stripes, providing you mow the lawn up and down alternately. A roller passing over the grass as it is cut flattens the blades in the mowing direction, creating a stripe.

If you choose to collect your grass clippings, value them and use them to improve your soil

A mower is not the only essential: a few other tools and bits of equipment will be required if you are to keep the lawn in good shape.

What size mower should I choose?

Mowers are available in a range of cutting widths: the wider the mower, the less time it takes to cut the grass! This is a rough guide to suitable cutting widths:

- Small garden: 30–42cm cutting width
- Medium garden: 42–52cm cutting width
- Large garden: more than 55cm cutting width

For large gardens it is worth considering a ride-on mower. A ride-on is generally less than double the price of a quality rotary mower.

Do I need to collect the grass clippings?

Grass clippings left on the surface of the lawn look unsightly and, as they decompose, damage the growing blades beneath them. They are also a nuisance when they are picked up on people's shoes and carried around the garden and into the house. If you do not wish to collect grass clippings, choose a mulch mower.

Mulch mowers These are increasingly popular. A mulch mower utilises a domed deck above the rotating blades. The grass cuttings are circulated in the dome, where they are chopped into smaller pieces before being forced down into the turf between the grass plants. They then quickly break down on the soil surface, releasing nutrients into the soil and increasing the organic content of the ground beneath the turf.

Modern mulch mowers work brilliantly if the grass is cut back by no more than one-third of the height of the grass blades. If grass is long, the process of making it shorter should be done in stages. Contrary to expectations, mulch mowing does not encourage moss and thatch; in fact, it helps to prevent the latter and encourages healthy grass development.

If you choose to collect your grass clippings, value them and use them to improve your soil (see pages 54–56).

What other equipment do I need?

Apart from a decent mower, there are some other tools that will be necessary, or useful, at some time during the year.

Good-quality, long-handled edging shears Some recommend trimming the edges of the lawn with a strimmer, others use a variety of mechanical edgers, but the most versatile, easy-to-use edging tool is a good-quality pair of long-handled shears. Cheap, poor-quality shears are false economy; they are often awkward and unpleasant to use and they do not last.

A spring-tine lawn rake A quality lawn rake with tines made of spring steel is essential for raking out moss and thatch (see page 31). Check that the tines are strong and springy before you buy. Curved, fan-shaped rakes, with a concave underside, are more satisfactory than flat, straight-ended ones.

A flat-tine plastic lawn lake This is the easiest way to collect leaves and debris from the lawn, or to rake up prunings and trimmings when tidying the border, without harming the grass. It is also useful for removing wormcasts.

A garden fork and spade The fork is the most convenient way of spiking the lawn to aerate it (see page 27). A sharp spade is the most versatile tool to straighten and sharpen lawn edges in spring. It is also necessary for planting bulbs and sorting out dips and bumps in the lawn.

Other useful tools...

● A watering can or sprayer, if you are using moss and weedkiller concentrates (see pages 31–32, 38).

● A hand trowel, to remove the odd weed and do repairs.

● A fertiliser spreader – essential for larger lawns (see pages 41–42).

● A mechanical lawn rake, if you have a perpetual problem with moss.

● A strimmer, if grass runs right up to walls, steps or fences. Use only with great care near trees (see page 58).

A half-moon edging iron Some gardeners favour this traditional tool for edging the beds. However, it is only useful on straight edges. Quality is essential: cheap ones soon bend and become useless.

A hose and lawn sprinkler A hose and sprinkler are essential for most lawns. Certainly if you are going to apply a granular lawn fertiliser it is unwise to rely on natural rainfall. A hose and sprinkler, used wisely, will keep the lawn green and attractive in short dry spells. The use of hoses and sprinklers may be restricted in drought conditions.

A wheelbarrow In all but the smallest gardens a wheelbarrow is essential for collecting leaves, debris, raked-out moss and thatch, as well as for applying lawn dressing – and just for moving tools around.

Composing

Unless a mulch mower is used, all lawns generate a lot of grass clippings during the growing season. These can be a valuable source of nutrients and organic matter, which can be used to condition and enrich the beds and borders used to grow flowers and vegetables. The secret of success is good composting practice.

Successful compost requires a mix of fresh green waste, such as grass clippings, and brown, woodier material, such as garden prunings and leaves.

My grass clippings go wet and slimy – why?

Fresh, moist grass clippings left alone in a heap will quickly degenerate into a moist, slimy mass. This is because there is little air space among the clippings and the composting process is the result of the activity of bacteria that work without oxygen. Bacteria of this type produce a lot of heat but the heap warms up and cools down quickly, producing a soggy, unpleasant mess.

Good-quality soil-conditioning compost is produced by bacteria that use oxygen. To encourage this process, it is vital to provide air space in the heap of grass cuttings by incorporating drier, more fibrous material. The composting process will be slower but more effective.

Successful composting needs:

● Air – for the bacteria that break down the decomposing material.

● Water – sufficient to aid the composting process.

● A variety of organic waste – if it rots, you can compost it.

To make good compost you need a variety of green and brown garden and kitchen waste. Kitchen waste should not include any cooked or meat products as these attract vermin.

Green waste includes grass clippings, annual weeds (preferably without mature seeds), light shrub clippings and prunings, vegetable and fruit peelings, faded cut flowers, faded garden blooms.

Brown waste includes fallen leaves, dry flower stems, light woody prunings, straw, dry grass stems and leaves.

Build up a heap of brown waste in preparation for the main grass-cutting season. Add a layer of brown waste after each layer of fresh green cuttings and other green waste. A compost heap built this way will produce lovely sweet compost in 12 months or so. Water the heap as you build it, especially if the grass clippings are dry.

Build up a heap of brown waste in preparation for the main grass-cutting season

A compost heap can be a simple affair. Here a timber frame covered in wire mesh contains the grass clippings and garden waste.

Do I need to add anything to speed up the composting process?

You do not have to add anything, but there are excellent accelerators that speed up the process. A sprinkling of pelleted poultry manure, for example, works well when added to each layer.

Do I have to have a compost container?

The point of using a container is to help keep the heap tidy and contained, and to retain heat, which accelerates the composting process. It also keeps in moisture but keeps out excess wet, which can cool the heap.

Above: A triple-bin compost enclosure is ideal. Below: Fresh grass clippings can be used to mulch mature shrubs.

Where space permits, have more than one compost heap. Three adjacent bins are ideal: one full of compost ready to use, one full and in the process of composting, and one being filled. In small gardens, a plastic or wooden container keeps things tidy and efficiently composts small volumes of grass clippings and garden waste.

Can I put grass clippings straight onto the garden?

Fresh clippings can be used as a mulch under mature shrubs and trees as long as they are not heaped up around the stems of the plants. Decomposing clippings produce heat. It is not a good idea to spread them around evergreens late in the season; the warmth could stimulate soft growth, which will be susceptible to frost damage.

Decomposing clippings take some nitrogen from the soil; initially this may slow the growth of young plants and cause yellowing of foliage.

Can I use clippings from a lawn treated with weed or moss killer?

You can compost the clippings from a lawn treated with weed killer, but do not use the compost for at least six months. It is not advisable to use these clippings as a mulch, except perhaps under a mature hedge such as laurel and only if there is no chance of them coming into contact with the foliage of the shrub.

Clippings from a lawn that has been treated with a moss killer based on iron sulphate can be safely used for composting in the normal way.

Trees in the lawn

The lawn is an ideal place in which to incorporate a tree, or trees, into the garden. They can be displayed as specimens, without competition from surrounding planting, and the natural shade provided by a tree's canopy creates a pleasant place to sit in summer. Sited in the lawn, a tree does not interfere with the growing conditions of other plants in the garden. However, it can have a profound effect on the grass beneath its canopy.

Positioning trees in the lawn

Trees planted as individual specimens, or in groups, in grass need careful positioning; their presence is much more obvious than when they are surrounded by shrubs and perennials. They should always be considered as part of the overall structure of the garden, viewed in relation to the rest of the planting.

A tree adds a new dimension to a lawn, transforming the open space with height and changing shadows.

Good trees to plant in lawns

... in small gardens

- Betula pendula 'Tristis'
- Crataegus persimilis 'Prunifolia'
- Malus 'Evereste'
- Sorbus 'Joseph Rock'

... in medium-sized to large gardens

- Betula utilis var. jacquemontii
- Eucalyptus pauciflora subsp. niphophila
- Liquidambar styraciflua 'Worplesdon'
- Malus hupehensis

Keeping a circle of ground free from grass around a tree helps the tree and makes mowing easier.

There is often a temptation to plant too near the boundaries of the garden and too close to the edges of the lawn. Allow trees to bring height into the central space of the garden and you make the picture much more interesting and more three-dimensional. A tree closer to the house provides height in the foreground, increasing the perspective and making the garden appear longer when viewed from the house. Trees positioned at strategic points in the garden become focal points, drawing the eye through the whole garden picture.

To make sure trees are planted in the right positions, use tall canes or stakes to mark the proposed positions, then view them from various points, including the upstairs and downstairs windows of the house.

It is also useful to take a few digital photographs of the garden and draw the proposed trees onto the pictures, or onto tracing paper laid over them, to give an impression of what they will look like when in position.

Growing trees in grass

- Keep a circle of ground around the trunk of newly planted and young trees clear of grass. This allows free passage of rainwater into the ground and prevents competition between the grass and the tree for water and nutrients.

- Consider how you will cut the grass at the base of the tree, especially immediately around the trunk. Avoid using strimmers, as they all too often cause damage to the bark, sometimes breaking right through to the living part of the wood. Repeated damage can result in the death of the tree. Likewise, careless use of mowers can cause major damage to trees of all ages. It is often more practical to keep a circle around the base of a tree permanently free of grass.

- Avoid trees whose roots tend to be close to the surface, such as ornamental cherries (Prunus), and those

that sucker, such as sumach (*Rhus typhina*). These will be a constant problem when mowing.

● Light, airy trees, such as birch (*Betula*) and gleditsia, cast only dappled shade and allow grass to grow successfully under their canopy as long as a grass mixture suitable for shade is used. Under heavier trees, such as Norway maple (*Acer platanoides*), beech (*Fagus sylvatica*) and oak (*Quercus robur*), it may be better to dispense with grass immediately under the tree and use bark chippings or gravel instead. Alternatively, plant low, shade-loving shrubs beneath the canopy.

Light, airy trees such as birch cast only dappled shade beneath their canopy. When a tree is grown directly in grass, take great care when mowing or strimming around it.

● Choose a tree that is appropriate to the size of the garden and the size of the lawn. All gardens have room for at least one tree.

● Young trees are often supplied with branches right down to ground level. These will need to be removed early in the life of the tree or they will be an obstacle when mowing the grass. Selective pruning of overhanging branches is best carried out an early stage, rather than waiting until they become a major problem and large limbs have to be removed.

● Standard trees, that is those with at least 2m (6ft) of clear stem, are the best choice for planting in lawns. Weeping trees are not a good idea, unless they are underplanted with low-maintenance ground-cover plants in an island bed.

Alternatives to grass under trees

In some cases it is just impossible to get grass to grow successfully under large mature trees, even when a seed mixture specifically for shade is used. In this situation it may be better to dispense with grass and introduce evergreen ground-cover planting that will extend the green space from the lawn under the canopy of the tree (see left).

Variegated forms of ground-cover plants are always valuable for adding light in the shady area beneath a tree.

The ground under a large mature tree will be dry, with the tree competing with any other plants for water and nutrients. Establishing new plants is always a challenge, but is possible if the right ones are chosen.

● Incorporate plenty of garden compost into the planting positions and keep new plants well watered until they start to make vigorous growth on their own.

Shrubs in lawns

Individual shrubs planted as specimens in lawns are not generally a good idea. Mowing around them is difficult, unless a sufficient area is kept free of grass at the base of each plant. Even then this can be a maintenance issue, as grass and weeds invade and grow up between the branches. As the shrubs grow, the plants become broader and overhang the lawn, getting in the way of the mower.

Isolated shrubs planted in the lawn look lost and unnatural in neatly maintained gardens where they are surrounded by closely mown grass. However, some subjects can be successfully incorporated in informal, roughly mown grass in more rural settings. Shrubs such as *Viburnum opulus, Philadelphus coronarius, Buddleja davidii, Syringa vulgaris* and varieties of cornus suit this naturalistic type of planting.

In larger gardens, shrubs planted in lawns are best in groups of three or five of one variety. The planting positions should be kept free of grass to start with; once established the shrubs will successfully withstand the competition.

Top left: *Cornus controversa* 'Variegata'. Above from the top: *Viburnum opulus, Philadelphus coronarius* 'Aureus', *Buddleja davidii* 'Royal Red', *Syringa vulgaris* 'Alba'.

Flowerbulbs in grass

Many flowerbulbs will grow well in grass, bringing valuable spring, and even autumn, colour to the green space of the garden. They are particularly successful under trees: often the grass is thinner here, and it is easier to leave it unmown so the bulb foliage can be allowed to die down naturally. Some flowerbulbs will establish and perform year after year, particularly if the planting situation is similar to their natural habitat.

Daffodils and narcissi are the bulbs most commonly grown in grass; they are robust plants and compete well with the grass. Many dwarf bulbs, including crocus, snowdrops, scillas and *Anemone blanda*, grow successfully in grass, but it has to be short if the flowers are to be seen.

Choosing narcissi for naturalising in grass

To create a natural effect, it is important to choose the right varieties. Frequently a mixture of daffodils and narcissi is used for 'naturalising', but this is not the best option. In the wild, plants distribute seeds around themselves, producing colonies of the same type. Wild daffodils, bluebells, wood anemones and snowdrops all grow naturally in this way; the impact and beauty lies in the volume of these drifts of a single flower type.

The effect is lost when mixed groups of bulbs are planted and a muddle of shapes, colours and heights results. Mixed bulbs will not all flower at the same time. This can prolong the flowering season, but in a clump of ten bulbs only two or three flowers may appear at any one time and the overall effect is sparse and has little impact.

Good narcissus varieties include...

● *Narcissus* 'February Gold' Dainty, bright yellow flowers early in the season.

● *Narcissus* 'Jetfire' Similar, but with a wonderful orange trumpet. Long-lasting, weather-resistant flowers.

● *Narcissus* 'Hawera' One of the latest; pale lemon, multi-headed flowers; thin, grassy foliage that presents few problems as it dies back.

● *Narcissus pseudonarcissus* The wild daffodil – a graceful narcissus with pale primrose petals and a golden trumpet.

● *Narcissus* 'Tête-à-tête' Probably the most popular dwarf narcissus, with charming yellow blooms. Weather-resistant and reliable; suited to short grass.

The rules for naturalising narcissi in grass

Clumps of yellow daffodils look glorious planted in a large drift under a spring-flowering cherry tree.

● Plant in groups or drifts of one variety; by all means use other varieties in other drifts, to extend the flowering period.

● Select appropriate varieties. Large-flowered and double narcissi do not lend themselves to naturalising in grass. Choose varieties that have smaller flowers and a more graceful habit.

● Let the leaves die down naturally, returning food to the bulb ready for next year's flowers. Areas of grass where the bulbs are planted cannot be mown until the bulbs' leaves start to yellow and wither.

● In smaller gardens, plant in clumps rather than in large, loose drifts. Leave enough space between the plantings to allow mower access.

Positioning bulbs in grass

Naturalised bulbs look best on the edge of grassed areas, around big shrubs or under trees. This is how related bulbs grow in the wild. The reason the plant produces bulbs in the first place is to give it a competitive edge early in the year. The bulb holds a reserve of water and food, so the plant can flower and set seed before the tree's leaves open and compete for nutrition.

A clump of bright yellow narcissi in flower will attract attention, becoming a temporary focal point in the garden. Take care not to position it near something you want to hide from view.

Planting bulbs in grass

● Plant bulbs deep enough and at the right distance apart. Plant at a depth of at least three times the bulb's height, and space bulbs the same distance apart as the bulb's diameter. Instructions on bulb packets often recommend planting farther apart, but this will result in very thin clumps or drifts, and a natural effect will not be achieved for several years, until the bulbs multiply.

The wild daffodil, *Narcissus pseudonarcissus*, is lovely in a naturalistic setting.

- Lift squares or rounds of turf, using a sharp spade. Cut around an area about 40cm (15in) in diameter and slip the blade of the spade under the turf to lift it. Put it to one side.

- Dig out a hole, placing the soil on a polythene sack laid on the grass, or in a bucket, to keep the grass clean. The hole should be about 15–30cm (6–12in) deep, depending on the size of the bulbs. This will take about ten standard-sized narcissus bulbs or 15 dwarf narcissi.

- Loosen the soil in the bottom of the hole and position the bulbs, nestling the base of each bulb into the prepared soil.

- Backfill the hole with soil and replace the turf. Gently firm the area with your foot. To prevent damage to the turf in wet conditions, it is a good idea to place a plank of wood over the turf before you firm it, then stamp on that.

- Group at least five of these plantings together to create a colony with impact.

Aftercare and mowing

Where bulbs are planted, the lawn can be cut in mild, dry weather up until midwinter; after this, the emerging shoots could be damaged by mowing. Keeping the grass cut short shows off short-stemmed bulb flowers to greater advantage.

Remember that you cannot cut the grass where the bulbs are growing until the foliage has died down; this may be as late as early summer.

The flowering performance of larger-flowered narcissi is improved by removing the seedheads after the flowers have faded, leaving the flower stalks intact to help to build the bulb's food reserves. The small-flowered narcissi can be left alone; they may seed under favourable conditions.

From the top: *Narcissus* 'February Gold', *Narcissus* 'Jetfire', *Narcissus* 'Canaliculatus', *Narcissus* 'Thalia'.

Other bulbs in grass

Tulips Tulips do not lend themselves to growing in grass. They are from warmer, drier regions of the world and the bulbs are not used to being under a damp lawn for much of the year. However, most will perform in their first season and, when grown in long grass, they can be used to enhance an area that has been planted to give the effect of a meadow. Single, strong-coloured varieties look best, perhaps the deep purple-black *Tulipa* 'Queen of Night' or the scarlet *Tulipa* 'Apeldoorn', to create a poppy effect. Their foliage, although large, dies down quickly.

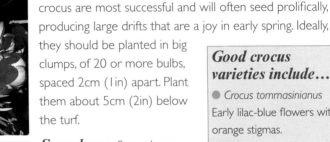

Crocus The small-flowered, narrow-leaved species crocus are most successful and will often seed prolifically, producing large drifts that are a joy in early spring. Ideally, they should be planted in big clumps, of 20 or more bulbs, spaced 2cm (1in) apart. Plant them about 5cm (2in) below the turf.

Snowdrops Snowdrops are lovely naturalised in semi-shade on soil that does not get too dry in summer. There are many choice varieties but the common single snowdrop, *Galanthus nivalis*, with its narrow, grey-green leaves, is the best to naturalise in grass. Plant the bulbs in early autumn; small and fragile, they deteriorate if stored too long. Plant in clumps of 10 or more, spaced 2cm (1in) apart, 6cm (2.5in) deep. The display is often sparse in the first year but improves as the bulbs establish and multiply.

> ### Good crocus varieties include…
>
> ● *Crocus tommasinianus* Early lilac-blue flowers with orange stigmas.
>
> ● *Crocus tommasinianus* 'Whitewell Purple' Very showy, with blue-purple flowers.
>
> ● *Crocus tommasinianus* 'Ruby Giant' Rich red-purple flowers with a lighter base.
>
> ● *Crocus chrysanthus* 'Gipsy Girl' Bright yellow flowers with bronze veining on the outside of the petals.

Autumn bloomers Some bulbs flower in autumn. They are best positioned where mowing can be avoided from midsummer onwards.

● Colchicums produce their lilac-pink, crocus-like flowers in autumn, before the leaves appear. They grow

From the top: *Crocus tommasinianus* 'Ruby Giant', *Crocus tommasinianus*, *Galanthus nivalis*.

successfully in grass, but be prepared for the large, luxuriant foliage that emerges in spring. The single *Colchicum autumnale* is the most successful variety.

Camassia leichtlinii is an ideal bulb to naturalise in grass under birch trees.

● The autumn-flowering saffron crocus, *Crocus sativus*, with its lilac-blue flowers and saffron-orange stamens, deserves wider planting. It likes well-drained soil and a sunny position.

● The autumn-flowering *Cyclamen neapolitanum* can be grown in thin grass, ideally around the base of a tree. It is charming in autumn, with pink or white flowers that precede the ivy-like silver and green marbled leaves.

Prairie effect In areas where the grass is left to grow until midsummer or beyond, there is the option of planting some exciting, more unusual flowerbulbs with taller stems.

● The honey-garlic *Nectaroscordum siculum* is a striking plant, with stems about 1m (3ft) tall and chandeliers of green, cream and ruby flowers that dry to attractive parchment seedheads.

● The quamash, *Camassia leichtlinii*, is a prairie native, with silver and green leaves and spikes of starry, sapphire flowers that reach a height of 60cm (2ft) or more in early summer.

Wildflower meadows

Gardening to establish native flora and fauna has become a way of life for many of us. We spend a small fortune on birdfood to encourage feathered friends into our garden. We attempt to garden organically, to prevent harm to wildlife and to encourage bees, butterflies and beneficial insects. We discourage the weeds but cherish wildflowers, sowing seed and planting native species.

Copying nature The wildflower meadow has become a popular design feature in gardens of all sizes but, contrary to popular belief, it is not an easier option than a fine lawn. Interestingly, many wildflowers prove difficult to establish in a garden situation and quickly die out rather than flourishing and multiplying as we had hoped, so results are often disappointing after the first season.

A garden is an artificial environment, where the natural balance has been interfered with by the gardener. To achieve long-term success with wild flora and fauna, you must reinstate balance into the ecosystem.

The first thing to consider is soil type and fertility. It is one of the primary considerations when choosing cultivated plants for our gardens, so why should it be any different with wildflowers? Natives of chalk downland, for example, are unlikely to thrive on richly fertile or moist, peaty soil. The secret of success is always to emulate the plant's natural environment.

Choosing the right wildflowers Wildflowers that will succeed in a meadow situation are those that are normally found in this habitat. These are plants that compete and grow in harmony with grasses. Plants such as poppies quickly die out as they like disturbed soil – hence their prevalence in grain fields and on wasteland. If you want them in your meadow, you may have to intervene and re-sow in areas where you have broken the soil. Clovers, vetches, buttercups and yellow rattle, on the other hand, reappear year after year with little problem.

Cutting: the key to success The key to success with any wildflower meadow is the cutting regime. We need to treat the meadow like a rural habitat that would have been cut for hay; this is the environment where meadow flowers thrive. Grass and flowers are allowed to grow through the spring and bloom through early summer. By late summer their seed is set and ripe. The meadow is

then cut, and everything is left on the ground to dry. Seed from flowers falls to the ground and all cuttings are then collected, as if hay were being made. The meadow is cut periodically in autumn and in early spring, as though grazed by animals; all clippings are removed at each cut. From mid-spring it is left to grow and bloom.

This wildflower meadow is a glorious sight in summer.

The removal of the grass and plant cuttings is vital. Left on the meadow, the clippings break down into the soil, increasing its fertility. This feeds the grass with more nitrogen, making it lush and thick and more competitive with emerging wildflower seedlings. Most native meadow flowers need low fertility and good drainage to thrive, and seed germination is impeded by increased fertility.

Your input A wildflower area requires your input. You will have to remove undesirables: docks, thistles and willow seedlings, for example. You may need to thin areas to open up soil space for seedlings to develop. You may need to aid the scattering and dispersal process, and you can of course increase the variety by introducing seed of other species.

A wildflower meadow without sowing

In large gardens on poor soil it is sometimes possible to establish a meadow without sowing. Normally when a garden has been uncultivated for a period of time, grass is left uncut for several seasons. The grass dies back in the winter and breaks down in the soil, increasing its fertility. This results in progressively stronger and lusher grass each spring. By cutting the grass in late summer, removing all the clippings, then keeping the grass short through to the following spring, you will gradually reduce this increase in the soil's fertility. Over a period of time, often only a year or two, the grass becomes thinner and finer, and wildflowers move in naturally, particularly in rural areas.

Bending the rules

A meadow effect can be achieved without grass by sowing a mixture of fast-growing, quick-to-flower annuals that grow well in colonies. These may be mixed or sown in drifts, and will create a gloriously colourful meadow in just a few weeks. You can buy a designer mixture blended for height or colour or you can make your own by blending suitable varieties.

This approach to meadows is ideal for sunny, dry borders with poor soil that may be planted at a later

From the top: Meadow flowers establish easily if the grass is cut and cleared from late summer onwards. Common spotted orchid. Common red clover.

date, for example adjoining newly built houses. It is also ideal alongside a more traditional grass area, perhaps as a transitional zone between grass and planting or grass and hedge, particularly in a rural area. Suitable plants to use include: opium poppy, cornflower, field poppy, cosmos, eschscholzia, flax, fairy toadflax, red clover, corn marigold and annual rudbeckia.

Establishing a meadow

The following steps to establish a meadow apply whether you are using a native wildflower and grass meadow mix or a blend of annuals to give a meadow effect. As with all planting, good ground preparation reaps rewards – although in this case we are not trying to improve the fertility of the soil.

● Dig over the soil, ideally to the depth of the blade of a spade, in autumn. Leave the ground rough over winter and allow the frost to break down the soil further. Do not add any compost or fertiliser.

● Rake over the plot in early spring to produce a level seedbed. Water if dry and leave for three weeks or so. Weed seeds will germinate prolifically. These can be hoed off and removed or, if you prefer, killed with a contact, non-residual weed killer. Any perennial weeds should be left and spot treated with a glyphosate-based weed killer.

● When the ground is clear, sow the seed mixture. To get even results mark out a grid of 1m (3ft) squares, using sand sprinkled onto the ground, and sow one square at a time. For a more natural look, mark out drifts with the sand and sow different varieties or mixtures in each drift.

● Remove any obviously undesirable weeds as they germinate. Re-sow any thin areas and thin out any overcrowded areas. In small meadows you can transplant at this stage to achieve a more even effect.

Note... If the site has been badly infested with weeds in the past there will also be plenty of weed seeds to germinate. In these circumstances it may be better to start again with a fresh sowing of seeds each spring, perhaps saving seed from the plants the previous summer before the meadow is cut down.

● Normally the area is past its best by late summer. Cut it down with a strimmer, or a rotary mower on the highest setting if this is easier, leaving the cut plant material on the soil surface. This will dry, dropping seeds onto the ground.

● Remove cuttings after a few weeks and lightly cultivate the area, removing any obvious weeds. The seeds are in the soil ready to re-grow the next spring.

Creative mowing

A neatly cut fine lawn with immaculate stripes: the grass in your garden does not have to be like this. With a little imagination you can transform the appearance of the grass just by mowing it differently, and perhaps cutting it to different lengths. Think of the grass like the gravel and stones in a Japanese garden: by raking them into different patterns, you can alter the garden dramatically without changing the constituent parts of the landscape.

Stripes are created by the direction of mowing. Changing the direction changes the pattern.

The effect of stripes Stripes on a lawn are created by the direction of mowing and are accentuated by the roller, if the mower has one. The lines created on the lawn lead the eye – normally down the garden, because this tends to be the most obvious way to mow.

If you change the mowing direction, perhaps so it goes diagonally, the eye may be directed to a different point in the garden. The most important thing to remember is that you do not always have to mow the lawn in the same direction.

Mowing in circles Where there are round, elliptical or oval beds in a lawn, you can adopt a circular mowing pattern. Mow around the beds, following their lines, in ever-increasing circles to a point more than halfway between two beds; repeat around other beds until mowing circles overlap and the whole area is covered. The end result should resemble the ripples radiating from stones thrown into a pool.

Varying the length of grass You do not have to cut all the grass in the garden to the same height. You can make a large expanse of grass more interesting by cutting some areas short and leaving others longer. The different areas will be different shades of green and will vary in texture. In large gardens this regime also means you will lighten the weekly workload because the longer grass will not have to be cut so frequently.

Mown paths lead through the tall-growing grass and flowers of a meadow.

The variation in length can be dramatic: a finely cut, manicured lawn can border directly onto a more informal area of long grass under trees. Or you can create a more subtle effect by mowing part of the lawn short, perhaps to a height of 3cm (1in) or so, and maintaining a shaped area at a height of around 6–8cm (2.5–3in). The shape of this area could follow that of the lawn or perhaps echo the shape of a large planting area. The overall effect will be to break up the expanse of solid green and make the area of grass interesting to look at.

Paths through grass In large gardens and paddocks, an informal area can be designed purely with the mower. Paths mown through long grass work in the same way as paths between flowerbeds and borders: they lead the eye, inviting exploration; they provide access; and they break up the mass of planting. If you start mowing paths in mid-spring, you will be able to watch the design develop as the grass grows. The expanse is also broken up by the variations in colour: the mown paths remain green while the longer grass flowers and then gradually turns to straw.

Lush grass on fertile soil is effective when kept long early in the season but it tends to collapse in heavy rain once the grasses are in full flower. Fine, sturdy grasses on less fertile soil tend to maintain the effect for longer.

Choosing the right mower It is important to choose a mower that can cope with long grass. Wheeled rotary mowers are a good option, but it is wise to ask the advice of a specialist garden machinery dealer.

You can collect the clippings; if your mower has a grassbox it will fill up quickly and need regular emptying. Alternatively, use a mower with a side discharge facility. As the grass is cut, it is thrown to the side of the mower and piles up in a long strip, like those you see during haymaking. Leave this to dry a little before raking it up and removing it for composting (see pages 54–56).

Lawncare blueprints

The following pages summarize two lawncare regimes. The first is the least you can get away with if you are to keep your lawn looking attractive all year and in good enough condition to withstand average use in summer. The second should enable you to achieve an immaculate lawn, as long as you give it regular attention. This need not be arduous but it must be consistent throughout the seasons.

The bare-minimum regime

Autumn...

● This is the most important time of the year in lawncare: you need to help the grass recover after the wear-and-tear of summer and get ready for winter.

● Apply a granular fertiliser and moss killer in mid-autumn (see page 32).

● Rake out blackened areas of moss after two weeks.

Winter...

● Rake up leaves periodically.

● If the grass keeps growing: in mild weather mow the lawn with the mower on the highest setting – this will collect any fallen leaves at the same time.

Note... Although this regime should keep the lawn looking good, a more thorough overhaul every three or four years will rejuvenate the lawn (see pages 26–29) and will be well worth the effort.

Early spring...

● Start cutting the lawn regularly, at least fortnightly.

● Spike any bare patches of grass, or areas where the soil feels hard and compacted, with a garden fork.

● Apply lawn dressing to bare patches and thin areas (see pages 28–29) and oversow lightly with a grass seed to suit your particular lawn.

Mid-spring...

● Tackle lawn weeds using a selective lawn weed killer.
(see pages 36–38).

● Keep cutting regularly. If the weather is warm and the
grass is growing quickly, start cutting once a week. If it is
cool, cut once a fortnight.

Late spring and summer...

● Tackle weeds as they appear with a ready-to-use
weed killer (see pages 36–38).

● Mow regularly, once a week. Regular mowing is much
easier, and takes less time, than less frequent mowing.

● To green-up the lawn, apply a low-nitrogen feed
designed for regular feeding (see page 41) after cutting

● Depending on local restrictions, use a lawn sprinkler
in dry weather to help keep the lawn green. Children will
enjoy it too!

Note... Perhaps you
moved to a new home with
a beautiful, well-groomed
lawn and then, in the early
days of summer, the lawn
started to deteriorate?
This may be because for
the previous owners the
lawn was to look upon
and to walk upon, but now
it is very much a surface
to play upon. This change
of use will require extra
input from you during the
recovery period.

The ideal regime

Early autumn...

● Apply a combined autumn lawn feed and moss killer as soon as the soil is moist enough (see page 43).

● Tackle any lawn pests such as leatherjackets or chafer grubs (see page 46).

Mid-autumn...

● After two weeks scarify the lawn to remove dead moss and thatch. Then spike the lawn using a lawn aerator or garden fork. (See pages 26–27.)

● Apply a lawn dressing evenly across the lawn after the grass has been given a light cut (see pages 28–29). Oversow bare and thin patches with grass seed and rake into the dressing. If it has turned cold, leave this until spring.

● Continue to mow every two weeks or so until the grass stops growing – if it does.

● Collect leaves regularly and remove from the lawn.

Remember the rule... Never remove more than one-third of the grass blades. If the grass is long, reduce the height gradually.

Winter...

● Continue to collect any leaves that fall and lie on the lawn.

● Mow the grass in mild weather, reducing the height by no more than one-third.

● Watch out for moles and implement control at the first signs of an invasion (see page 48).

● Get your mower serviced ready for spring.

Remember... You do not have to give the lawn every recommended feed and treatment every year. After a couple of seasons it will be easier to judge what you need to do and what gives the lawn that extra finish you are aiming for.

Early spring...

● Cut the lawn and apply a triple-action feed, weed and moss killer. Even application is essential, so use a lawn spreader carefully. (See pages 42–43.)

● Get the lawn edges into shape using a sharp spade or edging iron.

Mid-spring…

● Rake out any remaining moss and fill bare patches with lawn dressing oversown with grass seed. Keep these areas well watered until the grass is established.

● Cut the lawn regularly – ideally every ten days, or fortnightly if the weather is cool.

● Treat any remaining weeds with a selective lawn weed killer (see pages 36–38).

Late spring to early summer…

● Regular cutting is now the key to success. A weekly mow is quick and easy, and avoids cutting too much off the grass at once.

● Water the lawn in dry spells.

Early to midsummer…

● Continue to cut and water as necessary.

● Apply a slow-release granular lawn feed using a lawn spreader. Water regularly until the granules have completed disappeared. (See pages 41–42.)

Mid- to late summer…

Water the lawn in dry weather where permitted.

● To green-up the grass apply a low-nitrogen feed and conditioner (see page 41) after every three or four cuts.

● Mow regularly and tackle any invading weeds as they appear.

Index

Acknowledgments

The publishers would like to acknowledge with thanks all those
whose gardens are pictured in this book.

Picture credits

All photographs were taken by Andrew McIndoe with the
exception of:
Jane Sterndale-Bennett 55
Westland Garden Health 49
Front cover: Jonathan Buckley/The Garden Collection